WORLD RELIGIONS

AND

THE HOPE FOR PEACE

World Religions
and
the Hope for Peace

by

DAVID RHYS WILLIAMS

With a Preface by
JOHN HAYNES HOLMES

THE BEACON PRESS · BOSTON

Printed in U.S.A.

THIS BOOK IS DEDICATED

TO

LUCY ADAMS WILLIAMS

*who has graciously shared the responsibilities as well
as the rewards of the ministry;*

TO

FRANK ERNEST GANNETT

*who has faithfully supported the freedom of the pul-
pit during a ministry that must have often tried his
faith in such a freedom;*

AND TO

DR. JOHN R. WILLIAMS, SR.

*a friend but not a relative, who as physician has
abetted the calling of the ministry by calling in the
minister as an indispensable ally in the art of healing.*

WONDER OF WONDERS

Wonder of Wonders
Is the Holy Mystery
Enshrining the Birth of every Christ-Child!

Brave Akhnaton, prophet of purified religion,
Wise Confucius, benevolent counsellor of the people,
Saintly Mo Ti, the consistent exemplar of love,
Compassionate Gautama, proclaiming the sacredness of all life,
Far-visioned Isaiah, humble servant of the God above all nations,
Heroic Zoroaster, crusading champion of righteousness,
Penitent Asoka, anxious to atone for an unjust war,
Mystic Francis, gentle brother to both man and beast,
And lowly Jesus, Prince of Peace
And Herald of heaven on earth!

Whence came these Holy Saviors?
Whence these embodiments of Moral Genius?
What Mystic Spirit sired them?
What Cosmic Womb conceived them?
What Spiritual Omen presaged their advent?

Were they not Sons of Giant Meteors,
Progeny of the Milky Way,
Sparks from far-off Suns and Stars
Come to illumine Earth's Spiritual Night?

Who sent them here?
What brought them here?
Man Wonders!
Man will never cease to Wonder!

Contents

Contents

Foreword

THIS BOOK ATTEMPTS TO SUMMARIZE what is unique and what is universal in the various world religions. The point of view is that of a religious liberal frankly more concerned with positive appreciation than negative criticism.

The purpose has been to discover, if possible, a common spiritual dynamic as the basis of world understanding and cooperation.

The biographical approach seemed to offer the more vital and interesting introduction to what the world has really cherished and truly worshipped. In quoting the sacred scriptures of the particular faith under discussion in each chapter, the author has selected translations with a view to their clarity and cogency and in some cases has made free use of adaptations. He is greatly indebted to Mr. Alfred Stiernotte for valuable suggestions and for his services in verifying all references.

It is the contention of the author that there are enough common elements in the religions of mankind to enable the nations of the world to understand one another's systems of values, and to lay upon them the moral obligation to keep on striving for a just and durable peace until such peace is achieved.

DAVID RHYS WILLIAMS
Gannett House, Rochester, N. Y.

Preface

A COMBINATION OF QUALITIES makes this book an interesting and highly useful treatise in the field of comparative religion.

Thus, the author has chosen to tell his tale in terms of the lives and teachings of the major prophets of mankind. Writing in the conviction of Thomas Carlyle, that "universal history . . . is at bottom the history of the great men who have worked here," he has sought the religion of each separate country, or people, in the biographies of the supreme spiritual geniuses which they have produced. It is from this point of view that he discusses China in the persons of Confucius, Lao-tse, and Mo Ti; India in the transcendent achievements of Buddha and Gandhi; Greece in Socrates, as Rome in Marcus Aurelius, and the great Arab world in Mohammed. Jesus finds his place not apart from, but in the ranks of the august succession of the outstanding religious leaders of the past. This method of procedure will stir objection and dispute among the radicals of our time who contend that history, both sacred and secular, is fashioned not by persons but by forces. That the great impersonal factors of experience determine the destiny of men! But this characteristic aberration of our time leads us far astray, and is already become a waning influence among us. It is persons that count. "Thoughts that dwelt in the great men sent into the world," says Carlyle again, "[become] the soul of the whole world's history."

Secondly, Dr. Williams has wisely undertaken to present his story in simple terms, well calculated to invite popular reading on a wide scale. It is easy to write, on a subject of this kind, with vast display of erudition. The temptation to be expansively profound is well-nigh irresistible. Dr. Wil-

liams, himself a scholar, has yet had the genius to present the
very quintessence of his study and research. The result is a
book which may be trusted in every line, and yet be read
with sheer delight. Why are there not more books of this
type? Should not an author himself condense and illuminate
his own material, rather than leave this highly important
task to readers ill-prepared?

Lastly, this book is a tract for the times. By this I mean that
Dr. Williams's work is invariably made relevant to the events
of the passing hour. "In each chapter," he writes me in a
private letter, "I try to make a modern application of the
principles discussed." What is our need today but a return
to religion? And what is religion but the spiritual embodi-
ment of the triumphant faith in the love of God and man?
We perish if we find not brotherhood and peace. And here,
in the teachings of these prophets, do we find unanimous
accord in this gospel of the spirit. "Have we not all one
father? Hath not one God created us? Why do we deal
treacherously every man against his brothers?" This is spoken
not only by the Jewish prophet, Malachi, but by all these
prophetic voices. It is not a clash of contention that we hear
in these succeeding pages, but one great chorus of accord.
They agree, these religious teachers, and therewith hold the
key to life.

These are the qualities which combine to make this book
so worthy of attention. It is being published at just the right
moment — when it can do the most good. Religion has not
many voices, but only one. Let us listen — and follow on.

JOHN HAYNES HOLMES

WORLD RELIGIONS

AND

THE HOPE FOR PEACE

I

The Reasonableness of Confucius

The ancients when they wished to exemplify illustrious virtue throughout the empire, first ordered well their states. Desiring to order well their states, they first regulated their families. Wishing to regulate their families, they first cultivated themselves. Wishing to cultivate themselves, they first rectified their purposes. Wishing to rectify their purposes, they first sought to think sincerely. Wishing to think sincerely, they first extended their knowledge as widely as possible. This they did by investigation of things.

By investigation of things, their knowledge became extensive; their knowledge being extensive, their thoughts became sincere; their thoughts being sincere, their purposes were rectified; their purposes being rectified, they cultivated themselves; they being cultivated, their families were regulated; their families being regulated, their states were rightly governed; their states being rightly governed, the empire was thereby tranquil and prosperous.

— CONFUCIUS

THE PURPOSE OF THIS STUDY in comparative religion is to understand more fully the ideals and motivations of the various peoples of this earth with whom we have to cooperate if we are going to live together in peace and harmony in one world. We propose to compare not our profession of ideals with their practice, but our profession with their profession and our practice with their practice.

We begin with the religions of China, not because they are

3

the oldest, but because of the sudden rise of China to a position of strategic importance in international affairs. And we begin with Confucianism because it is by far the major religious influence in the life of the Chinese people. There is no religion that is being more faithfully practiced by those who profess it than is Confucianism.

There is no doubt that Communism —in coming up against Confucianism — is obliged to compete with one of the most deeply-rooted and comprehensive ideologies in the world today; and each is bound to be greatly modified by the other. The outcome will be interesting to watch because it will profoundly affect the future course of history not only for China but for the rest of mankind.

To understand Confucianism, it is first necessary to know something about its founder, who was one of the greatest but also one of the most prosaic personalities of all time, whose life and teachings are about as thrilling as the multiplication table, but, by the same token, as vital and important.

It is doubtful if such a personality as Confucius could have arisen to age-long prominence in any country save China, and this is not meant as anything but a high compliment to the Chinese people, and as something of a reflection on the rest of us.

In spite of the fact that the story of his life is barren of dramatic and colorful incident, Confucius was truly a religious genius of the first magnitude.

There is no sudden conversion to relate such as that of Paul on the way to Damascus, Buddha under the Bo-Tree, or Moses before the burning bush.

There is no story of extreme asceticism to pique our interest such as that of John the Baptist living on locusts and wild honey, Saint Simon standing on a pillar of stone for weeks and months at a time, or Francis of Assisi flagellating his body until it ran with blood.

There is no spectacular triumph to which to point such as Christ's entry into Jerusalem, Mohammed's capture of Mecca, or Elijah's contest on Mt. Carmel with the prophets of Baal.

There are no tales of magic and miracles to relate such as Aaron turning rods into serpents, Jesus turning water into wine, or Mary Baker Eddy healing the blind and the deaf, the lame and the halt.

There are no exaggerated claims to heavenly revelations to impress the multitude, such as Isaiah's experience with the cherubim in the temple, Socrates and the voice of his guardian angel, or Joseph Smith's discovery of the Golden Tablets.

There are no exciting prophecies of a Day of Judgment to come to arouse and capture the human imagination such as Christ's doctrine of the coming kingdom, Zoroaster's year of divine retribution, or Mohammed's final triumph of Allah.

There are no passages of sustained eloquence and lyrical beauty in the writings which he left behind such as we find in the prophecies of the Second Isaiah, the Jewish Book of Psalms, the Hindu Scriptures, or even in the writing of Laotse, a Chinese contemporary.

No, nothing of this kind exists at all in the biography of Confucius. We must content ourselves with the plain unvarnished story of a practical philosopher and statesman, who was more like America's Benjamin Franklin than anyone else (or Dr. Samuel Johnson who compiled the English dictionary), who was gifted with a high degree of common sense and a sustained drive to serve his fellow-countrymen, with intelligence and without fanaticism.

His biography must ever remain a brief one. His greatness lies in his teachings — and the greatness of these teachings lies in their intrinsic content and not in their literary form.

Confucius or K'un-fu-tze was born about the time of Buddha, 551 B.C., in the little state of Lu which is part of the modern province of Shantung which the Japanese tried to take from China at the close of the First World War and did succeed in overrunning during World War II. The father of Confucius was a poor man but respectably poor because he was of renowned lineage. His mother, however, was the greatest factor in his development.

We know nothing about the early life of this man, except that at fifteen years of age his mind was bent on learning. At nineteen he was married to a woman who bore him an only son. She was very much like Xantippe, the wife of Socrates — more or less out of sympathy with her husband's way of life.

At twenty-two years of age, he had become an expert on the wisdom of the ancients and began to attract a large following of students, until at one time there were three thousand coming to him daily for instruction.

Confucius was a born scholar and teacher. For many years he spent much of his energy in collecting and editing the ancient writings of his people which he published in five volumes called the Five kings: *Yih-king,* Book of Philosophy; *Shu-king,* Book of History; *Shi-king,* Book of Poetry; *Li-ki-king,* Book of Ceremonies; and the *Ch'un-ts'iu* (Spring and Autumn Annals), chronicles of the principality of Lu. These constitute the Old Testament in the sacred scriptures of Confucianism, the New Testament being composed of four books on the life and teachings of Confucius. These four classics are the *Lun-yü,* Conversations of Confucius (known as the "Analects" through a whim of the translator, Legge); the *Ta-hioh,* or the Great Teaching; the *Chung-yung,* or the Doctrine of the Mean; and *Meng-tsze,* the teaching of the philosopher Mencius. None of these was written by the master himself but all by his disciples.

At fifty years of age this scholar and teacher was called upon to give up his teaching and apply his principles to political affairs. He was made Minister of Justice in his native state of Lu, and such was the wisdom and efficiency of his administration that in a very short time the whole province became a model state. Crime ceased almost altogether. Learning became the major concern of the people, and prosperity greatly increased.

Confucius regulated everything from the diet of babies to the size of coffins, and created such a spirit of loyalty to the commonweal that officials in large numbers came flocking from other communities to sing his praises and seek his counsel.

He instituted a jury system to give justice to the common people. He preached honesty and benevolence to those in positions of authority. He inspired the entire citizenship with the duty of living righteously and peacefully. He laid down the principle that governments exist for the people, not the people for their governments. And he set an example by giving his services to his country without remuneration.

He became, of course, the hero of the hour and the idol of his people for a brief time thereafter. And then, all of a sudden, he was unceremoniously dismissed from office, due to the jealousy of the governor who had originally pleaded with him to become the Minister of Justice.

Compelled by feelings of pride and resentment rather than because of banishment, he wandered about for thirteen years, tramping from city to city and from province to province, seeking out some adventurous ruler who would employ his political abilities, offering to set his state in reasonable order within a period of three years at least — and all without remuneration. But, curiously enough, there was no ruler with sufficient imagination to take advantage of this offer.

It was during this period that his mother, his wife, his son and two of his more faithful disciples died, the loss of whom he grievously mourned. Perhaps he did not mourn so deeply the loss of his wife, although he had treated her with considerable kindness while living and ordered that due honor and respect be paid her on the occasion of her funeral.

At last there came a time when he could wander no longer. He came to the conclusion that to be wronged is nothing unless you continue to remember it. So, swallowing his pride, he reluctantly returned to his native province of Lu, determined to forget every injury done him, and there to die of a tired heart at the age of seventy-three.

> The great mountain must crumble;
> The strong beam must break;
> The wise man must wither away like a plant.[1]

These were his last words. Apparently it was difficult for him to forget the wrong which had been done to him.

Immediately after his death, however, Confucius began to grow in power and fame. His disciples came in great numbers to build their huts near his grave, and to this day, the encampment of faithful disciples has never completely broken up — even during the last two world wars. His tomb is now the center of a beautiful park lined with stately cypress avenues and covered with tablets erected to his memory; or at least it was so until the coming of the recent Communist uprising in that country.

His proverbs and sayings were carefully gathered together by three faithful disciples, the most famous being Mencius, who was born about one hundred years after his master's death.

It is interesting to note the gradual exaltation of Confucius from the status of a mere man, however wise, to the rank of complete divinity. In the year 1 A.D. he was canonized as the Duke Ni, The All Illustrious One; in 57 A.D. it was ordered that annual sacrifices be offered up to him at all colleges and universities; in 555 A.D., temples were erected to his memory; in 1068 A.D., he was raised to the rank of Eternal Emperor; in 1907 A.D. he was officially promoted to the highest pinnacle of worship, being equated with the Deity of Heaven and Earth.[2]

Strange, is it not, that a man who had so little use for ecclesiasticism as Confucius should have fifteen hundred temples erected in his name and something like sixty thousand animals sacrificed to his spirit every year! And stranger still that anyone so humble as to discourage any comparison between himself and the sages before him should ever become the object of a whole nation's prayer and worship!

What is the reason for this homage and veneration? Wherein lies its psychological basis? We must find it largely in the teachings of this man and their adaptability to the Chinese temperament rather than in the personality of the man himself. Let us therefore turn to a consideration of these teachings, which I shall present to you under seven main headings.

First of all in importance was his formulation of the Golden Rule, which he announced to the world fully five hundred years before the Christian era. A certain disciple inquired of the Master, "Is there one word which may serve as a rule of practice for all one's life?" "Yes," replied Confucius, "is not *reciprocity* such a word?" And then he went on to say, "Do not unto others what you would not want done to yourself."

Now some critics take delight in calling attention to the negative form of his Golden Rule — "Do not do" — overlooking the positive implications in the word *reciprocity* itself, which forms a part of the original. At any rate, it will be to the everlasting credit of Confucius that he was the first to enunciate the Golden Rule in any form.

The second point in his teachings was his emphasis on the sacredness of work. He did not encourage people to look forward to a period when they might retire from their labors. He believed and taught that work instead of being a curse is one of life's greatest blessings. One of his sayings which is read twice a month in all schools and colleges of China is, "Suffer no barren spot to remain a wilderness, nor a lazy person to abide in the town." It is no wonder that a country whose religion preaches the holiness of toil and the sinfulness of sloth should have built the largest canals and the biggest stone walls, the most enduring bridges, of any people; that it should have invented the mariner's compass, the printing-press, used smallpox antitoxins and anesthetics, discovered gunpowder and the circulation of the blood, and developed the silk and porcelain industries to a high degree of efficiency.

The third point was his stress on the leadership of the educated. "Learn the past," he declared, "and you will know the future. . . . With a mirror of brass you can adjust your hat, but with antiquity for a mirror you can predict the rise and fall of empires." He proceeded to gather the wisdom of the past in order that men might mold their future. To study the past without trying to find guidance for present conduct is a waste of time. He insisted that a knowledge of this wisdom should be the chief test of one's right to civic office and leadership, and, to this day — unless the recent revolution has made a drastic change — the real political power of China still resides in the hands of its educated citizens. It is an aristocracy not of birth as in England, nor of military power as in prewar Germany, nor of priestly privilege as in ancient Egypt, but a literary aristocracy which is open on equal terms to the humblest citizen's son. Handi-capped for centuries by a cumbersome alphabet, which has only recently been improved, the Chinese people as a whole have admired the scholar and philosopher above all other professions. They have insisted that their political leaders pass civil service examinations before permitting them to undertake positions of power and responsibility. This un-doubtedly has been the chief reason for the long continuity of China's civilization. There have been temporary indi-vidual usurpers and conquerors, but no hereditary bureau-cracy has been saddled on the people for any length of time. The teaching of Confucius concerning the leadership of the educated has always come to the rescue of the Chinese people sooner or later. And we may well have faith that whatever changes the new regime in China may be planning, it is not likely to flout successfully this deep-seated tradition of Chinese culture.

The fourth point which Confucius stressed is the importance of this life here and now. He preached the doctrine of "One world at a time." When asked about the question of immortality, he replied, "How can we know anything about death when we know so little about life? . . . To give oneself earnestly to the service of men, and while respecting the spirits to make no great to-do about them — that is wisdom," he declared. In this respect Confucianism is a wholesome antidote to all the other religions which hold this earth to be a vale of tears and life here something to be merely endured for the sake of a more abundant one hereafter. The religious liberals surely agree with Confucius on this point.

The fifth point in his teachings stressed the importance of reverential manners. He prescribed in elaborate detail the etiquette which should prevail between children and their parents, wives and husbands, brothers and sisters, employer and employee, citizens and public officials, and the living and the dead. Confucianism calls for three hundred different ceremonies and three thousand rules of behavior, all for the purpose of showing proper deference to whom deference is due. Perhaps the Chinese have taken Confucius too seriously in this matter of reverence and have exaggerated its importance to the point where it has been something of a handicap to their progress as a people. If this be so, then perhaps a strong dose of western disrespect is what they need, just as we ourselves could afford to import a little more of their way of reverence, especially concerning the aged and the learned.

The sixth point in the teachings of Confucius was his doctrine of the golden mean or, as he called it, "the doctrine of the middle road." "Nothing in extremes," he preached, "either in the matter of feasting or fasting, rejoicing or mourning, working or resting, spending or saving. . . . No extravagances in manner, conduct, speech or thought." Confucianism is above all else a religion of common sense and sanity, which gives the average citizen of China a certain poise and evenness that we hurried and strenuous westerners can well afford to emulate.

The final point of this religion to which I would call your attention is the founder's code of the five noble virtues. As Moses is famous for his Ten Commandments, Jesus for his nine Beatitudes, and Buddha for his Eightfold Path, so Confucius is known for his five noble virtues: dignity, generosity, mercy, tolerance, sincerity — and the greatest of these is sincerity. "Sincerity is the beginning and end of all things; without it there would be nothing." Every Chinese, even to this day, who considers himself a gentleman, wears five buttons on his coat, to remind himself and others of the five noble virtues which constitute true nobility of soul.

The golden rule of reciprocity, the blessing of work, the leadership of the educated, the wisdom of living one world at a time, the duty of reverence, the doctrine of the middle path, the five noble virtues — these constitute the sum and substance of Confucianism. What a highly ethical religion! How sane and reasonable! How practical and socially beneficial! Yes, and how humanistic!

With a minimum of theology, with the complete absence of magic and superstition as in the pure form in which it originated, and with a maximum of spiritual content, this religion is obviously very close to our own liberal point of view.

Confucianism is not known as such in China but simply as "the grand way — the superior way." It is interesting to note that Christianity was first known as "the Way." There are millions who openly profess loyalty to Confucianism, but there are many others who live by its teachings without knowing it.

In John Galsworthy's *The Flowering Wilderness* a young

British woman of culture inquires of her Tory uncle, "Are
you a Christian, Uncle?" "No, my dear," he replied, "if anything a Confucian. . . . Most of our caste in this country, if
they only knew it, are Confucian rather than Christian. Belief in ancestors and traditions, respect for parents, honesty,
moderation of conduct, absence of self-obtrusion." "What
more," murmured his niece, "does one want except the love
of beauty?" The uncle, of course, could just as well have
included the love of beauty among the Confucian characteristics, as the exquisite Chinese arts and crafts abundantly
attest.

Other religious leaders there have been who lived more
dramatically, preached more eloquently, and died less com-
plainingly than Confucius. But it would be difficult, if not
impossible, to find anyone in all history to outshine him in
honesty, in common sense, in humanitarian impulse, or in
sustained devotion to the common good.

If we of the West are in search of wisdom and would better
understand our neighbors on the other shore of the Pacific,
with whom we are destined to live in closer relations than
ever before whether we want to or not, then we should lose
no time in claiming their great sage and prophet as one of
our own and go to him, as we go to the Hebrew prophets and
Jesus, for counsel and religious inspiration.

May something of his moral integrity and firm loyalty to
the common good enter into our lives, that we too may be a
blessing to the age in which we live. May we, like him, search
for the truth which the past hath had, proving all things and
holding fast to that which is good.

2

Mo Ti and the Will to Peace

The Will of Heaven is to me what the compasses
and the try-square are to the artisan. The artisan
judges all circles and squares by his compasses and
try-square, saying "That which agrees with my standard is right, and that which does not agree is wrong."
Now there are teachers in our age who write numberless books and make numberless speeches, persuading
all classes of men from the princes to the student.
But they are all far from true love and righteousness.
I know it is so, because I have found the best standard
whereby to judge them.

— Mo Ti

Mo Ti, the Chinese saint, sage and saviour, was a founder
of a great religion, a religion comparable in its central message to Christianity and Buddhism, but a religion which has
been lost to the world for over 2,300 years, but which is now
being rediscovered and resuscitated by some of the scholars
and philosophers of China.

Mo Ti rises from his grave after 2,300 years to sound a
warning not only to the nations that border on the Pacific
but to all the nations of the earth.

Forgotten in his own land until very recently, there are
those who believe that Mo Ti is destined to take his place
among the chief sages of mankind, and his fame perhaps
eventually to spread throughout the world.

14

Mo Ti broke away from the old procedure best characterized in Lao-tse's own words:

> The world may be known
> Without ever crossing one's gate.
> Nor need one peep through the window
> In order Nature's cause to contemplate.
> The farther one goes,
> The less one knows.[1]

Direct observation was the method of Mo Ti. He belongs to that highest group of religious genius in which we would include the names of Isaiah, Jesus, Buddha, Akhnaton and King Asoka, but from which we would exclude the names of Mohammed and Zoroaster as these belong in a category somewhat less meritorious.

Probably no other important personage has been so neglected by the historians and the biographers. Professor Hu Shih, of the University of Peking, says, "Moh Tih, perhaps one of the greatest souls China has ever produced, has never had a biographer until the twentieth century."[2] With the exception of one small volume by Professor Hu Shih himself, there has been almost no attempt made to acquaint the English-speaking world with the message of one of the clearest thinkers in all history.

Mo Ti, the founder of Moism, was born about 500 B.C., in the same state in which Confucius was born. He lived for about eighty years, and died a natural death in spite of the fact that his teachings were officially held to be dangerous to the security of the Chinese Empire.

His central doctrine was *Love*. "The will of Heaven is to 'love all'," he said. Confucius saw nothing but impersonality behind the phenomena of the universe. But Mo Ti, like Hosea, Jesus and Akhnaton, put "Love" at the heart of things. The way of salvation for the world, therefore, was to practice love, he proclaimed. He said:

Leaders who wish to assume the responsibility of ruling the country should seek the prime source of unrest. It is lack of *mutual love.* Robbers love their own homes but not the homes of others, so they rob other homes in order to benefit their own. Dukes love their own dominions but not those of others so they disturb the others for the benefit of their own. Kings love their own countries but not others' and therefore fight with other countries for the sake of their own. The source of all this evil action is lack of mutual love. If all through the world people will regard the families of others as their own, who then will rob, steal or disturb? If Kings regard other countries as their own, who will fight? When there is mutual love, there is peace; when there is mutual hatred, there is war.[3]

Thus did he proclaim a gospel very similar to that of Christianity.

This doctrine of universal altruism constituted a repudiation of the Confucian principle of a gradation of love, the highest being reserved for one's parents and then decreasing with the remoteness of the relationship; the strongest being between the members of one's immediate family. Consequently, Mo Ti was accused of being an enemy of the family and patriotism, inasmuch as he wished to extend the family loyalty to everyone and patriotism to include every nation. He certainly was an enemy of that kind of patriotism which expresses itself in militarism.

Mo Ti, unlike Akhnaton, was not a thoroughgoing pacifist, because he *did* believe in the defense of one's country. What he opposed was offensive warfare. He declared:

Of all sins, attacking a country in war is the greatest. If people talk of morality and high virtues but do not try to abolish war they are concerning themselves with comparatively small things, not with essentials.[4]

There is a story told concerning Mo Ti which illustrates the intensity of his convictions on this matter. It seems that the army engineers of one of the Chinese kingdoms had developed a new device for scaling the walls of a beleaguered city, and the king of this particular kingdom, anxious to try out the new device, was preparing to attack a neighboring state. Mo Ti, hearing of this premeditated assault, started out from his dwelling place and traveled on foot for ten days and nights, arriving at the capital city exhausted but on time. He promptly sought an interview with the king and eventually, by his earnestness, dissuaded him from waging the intended war. The king said to him, "Before I met you, I had wanted to conquer the State of Sung. But since I have seen you I would not have it even if it were given me without resistance but with no just cause." To which Mo Ti replied: "If so, then it is as if I had already given you the State of Sung. Persist in your righteous course and I will give you the whole world."[5]

Some of you may be curious as to the type of argument which Mo Ti pursued with such success. Fortunately, it has been preserved for us. It constitutes the clearest ethical condemnation of war which I have ever read. It ought to be blazoned upon the walls of every school house and legislative hall in the world. Listen to the logic of a man who lived 2,300 years ago:

Here is a man who enters his neighbor's orchard and steals some peaches and plums therefrom. When this is known, he is condemned by the public, and when caught will be fined by the government. Wherefore? Because he has injured his neighbor to profit himself.

And if he steals from his neighbor a dog, a pig, or a chicken, he commits a wrong greater than the stealing of peaches and plums. Why? Because he has done a greater injury to another man; and the greater the injury he does, the greater the wrong, and the severer shall be his punishment.

And if he goes as far as to waylay an innocent man, take away his fur coat and cloak, and stab him with his sword, then his crime is still greater. . . . Why? Because he has done thereby a greater injury. And the greater the injury a man does to another, the greater is his crime, and the severer shall be his punishment.

In all these cases, the gentlemen of the world agree to condemn this man, and declare, "He is wrong."

Now there is the greatest of all crimes — the invasion of one nation by another. But the gentlemen of the world not only refuse to condemn it, but even praise it and declare, "It is right."

Shall we say that these gentlemen know the distinction between right and wrong?

Killing one man constitutes a crime and is punishable by death. Applying the same principle, the killing of ten men makes the crime ten times greater and ten times as punishable; similarly the killing of a hundred men increases the crime a hundred fold, and makes it that many times as punishable.

All this the gentlemen of the world unanimously condemn and pronounce to be wrong.

But when they come to judge the greatest of all wrongs — the invasion of one state by another — (which is a hundred thousand times more criminal than the killing of one innocent man) they cannot see that they should condemn it. On the contrary, they praise it and call it "right." . . . *Indeed, they do not know it is wrong.*

Here is a world which condemns a petty wrong and praises the greatest of all wrongs — the attack of one nation upon another — and calls it right. Can we say that the world knows the distinction between right and wrong? [6]

Would that Mo Ti were here today to quicken the conscience of the nations with a viewpoint on life for lack of which our modern civilization is approaching the precipice at whose base lies destruction!

Mo Ti not only proclaimed a gospel of Peace, and Love and Righteousness, but he proclaimed a religion of simplicity. He condemned outright the ornate and burdensome ritualism and formalism of his day. He proceeded to criticize Confucianism because it accepted the ancient institution of ancestor worship, which involved extravagant ceremonies for funeral and burial.

Above all, he rebelled against the scholasticism of the early Confucians because they refused to consider the practical consequences of beliefs and theories and institutions.

Hu Shih maintains that Mo Ti's main position is this: "that the meaning of every institution is what it is good for." These words sound like Christ's doctrine — "The Sabbath was made for man, not man for the Sabbath." Hu Shih also states further that "the meaning of every conception or belief or policy lies in what kind of conduct or character it is fitted to produce." ("By their fruits ye shall know them.")

Any principle which can elevate conduct should be perpetuated. That which cannot elevate conduct should not be perpetuated. To perpetuate anything that cannot elevate conduct is nothing but a waste of speech.[7]

Again we can draw the Christian parallel: "What doth it profit a man to gain the whole world but lose his own soul?" As Jesus rebuked the Pharisees of his day, so Mo Ti rebuked the Sophists of his day, saying,

They praise the *name* of righteousness, but do not recognize the *substance* of it. They may be likened unto a blind man who can define the names "black" and "white" as well as any seeing man, but who does not in practice differentiate between black and white.[8]

Mo Ti's remarkable clarity of thought is once more illustrated in the following passage:

Now a blind man may say, "That which shines with brilliancy is white, and that which is like soot is black." Even those who can see cannot reject these definitions. But if you place both white and black things before the blind man and ask him to choose the one from the other, then he fails. Therefore I say, "A blind man knows not white from black," not because he cannot name them, but because he cannot choose them.

Now when the gentlemen of the world undertake to define virtue and benevolence, even the wisest men of antiquity cannot surpass them. But if one takes a benevolent act and a malevolent act and asks them to choose the one from the other, then they fail. Therefore, I say, "The gentlemen of the world know not benevolence," not because of their definitions but because of their choice.[9]

How similar in viewpoint is all this to the observation of Jesus when he said: "Not all they who say 'Lord, Lord,' shall enter into the kingdom, but they that *do* the will of the Father who is in Heaven."

Also like Jesus, Mo Ti made a strenuous effort to practice what he preached. Important as his doctrines were, the life he lived was even more important. We do not need to take the word of his disciples for this, but we have the testimony of his adversaries. For Mencius, who was a follower of Confucius and a zealous critic of Mo Ti, was inspired nevertheless to express his admiration as follows: "Mo Ti loved *all* men and would gladly wear out his whole being from head to heel for the benefit of mankind." [10]

Another critic, Chuang-Tse, was moved to write:

The life of the Mohists is toilsome and their death ritual is too simple. . . . Their way is difficult to practice. . . . It is against human nature and man cannot stand it. Though Moh Tze himself could bear it how about the world? . . . But Moh Tze was certainly a glory to the world. What he could not attain he would never cease to seek, even though it be in privation and destitution. Ah, what a genius he was! [11]

Yes, he was a genius. A religious genius of the first magnitude, but altogether too far in advance of his time. His movement flourished for a time, but after three centuries it was almost completely wiped out by persecution because its ideals did not fit into the imperialistic tendencies of that age. Moism did not have any Constantine to give it prestige and protection. Its books were burned, its temples destroyed, and its adherents scattered. It died a martyr's death, even though Mo Ti himself was allowed to live to a ripe old age.

His ideas and ideals, however, have undergone an amazing renaissance in China in recent years. The Moist Sacred Scriptures, consisting of fifty-three books, are being read and studied with fresh enthusiasm after the long neglect of many centuries. The youth of that land are discovering that they too once had a Christ whom their fathers rejected. And what a timely discovery it is! As Occident and Orient groom themselves to contend for the domination of the Pacific, two voices from the distant past coming down through the many centuries and from opposite directions unite today in a common warning. The language is different but their essential message is the same. One says, "They that take the sword shall perish by the sword." The other says,

Mutual love is righteousness but warfare is unrighteousness. The former is beneficial to Heaven, spirit, country and humanity — the latter means destruction to all.[12]

May the spirit of Jesus and that of Mo Ti unite to preside over the destiny of the Pacific.

3

Lao-tse and the Inner Life

How do I know that love of life is not a delusion after all? How do I know but that he who dreads to die is not as a child who has lost the way and cannot find his home?

Once upon a time, I, Chuang Tze, dreamt I was a butterfly, fluttering hither and thither, to all intents and purposes a butterfly. I was conscious only of following my fancies as a butterfly, and was unconscious of my individuality as a man. Suddenly, I awaked, and there I lay, myself again. Now I do not know whether I was then a man dreaming I was a butterfly, or whether I am now a butterfly dreaming I am a man.

[By the same token] comes the Great Awakening, and then we find out that this life is really a great dream. Fools think they are awake now, and flatter themselves they know if they are really princes or peasants. Confucius and you are both dreams; and I who say you are dreams, — I am but a dream myself. This is a paradox. To-morrow a sage may arise to explain it; but that to-morrow will not be until ten thousand generations have gone by.

— *The Works of* CHUANG TZE

LAO-TSE, AN OLDER CONTEMPORARY of both Confucius and Mo Ti, was the alleged founder of modern Taoism.

I say alleged founder of Taoism advisedly, because Lao-tse had no more idea of founding a new religion than had Henry Thoreau or Ralph Waldo Emerson, with both of whom he may be likened in character and philosophical point of view. The religion that was founded around his writings and personality, fully six centuries after his death, had about as little connection with the historical Lao-tse as modern voodooism and the serpent-handling cults in this country have to do with the moral grandeur that was Jesus and his Sermon on the Mount.

In the second century, A.D., an upstart local war lord by the name of Chang Tao-lin, with a keen ambition to conquer all of China and found a new imperial dynasty, decided that a new religion was necessary to capture the imagination of the people and help him in solidifying his military gains.

So he deliberately borrowed the commanding figure of Lao-tse, who had lived seven centuries earlier, and took the one prose poem which this philosopher had written and made it the basis of a new set of sacred scriptures. He then mixed in generous amounts of myth, magic and superstition, taken from pre-existing popular polytheistic cults, with the results that we have in Taoism one of the weirdest concoctions of sense and nonsense ever to pass as a religion.

If you want to get a rough idea of what it is like, imagine some American Hitler or Huey Long arising in the future, taking the dignified figure of Ralph Waldo Emerson and draping it with half a dozen rattlesnakes and worshipping him as God Almighty, and then interpreting his famous Divinity School address on the Over-Soul with the ritual of voodoo, the rain incantations of the Navajo Indians, the strange antics of the Holy Rollers, and the mumbo-jumbo of those who believe in hexing and the Evil Eye. Then you have a fairly accurate picture of modern Taoism.

Of course we of the West never could become victims of such a gross and palpable fraud, or couldn't we? Competent historians have known for a long time that much of what has passed for Christianity was just such a synthetic product. The simple ethical gospel of Jesus was generously mixed with large portions of Greek philosophy and fragments of pagan mythology and superstition taken over from the numerous polytheistic cults which flourished throughout the Roman Empire in the centuries immediately before and after the time of Jesus; and this it was which became historical Christianity. We may well be grateful today that such a fabrication took place, otherwise, the moral grandeur of Jesus and his gospel might have been lost to the world forever. If it had not been for this protective covering of pagan superstition, the central core of the Christian ethics would have disappeared a long time ago.

By the same token, we may well be grateful to Taoism for preserving the august figure of Lao-tse from an undeserved oblivion that otherwise might have been his fate. For while Lao-tse was still held in remembrance when he was taken over by the religion builders, his remembrance was confined to philosophical circles.

Taoism today is the religion of the ignorant and illiterate among the Chinese, as Confucianism and Moism are the religions of the educated and intelligent. But there are forty-three million of them, nearly twice the number of Roman Catholics in America; they constitute a large enough group to be reckoned with. And not all of them are ignorant and superstitious by any means. There are numerous sects in Taoism, as in Christianity, and some are nearer to the point of view of its alleged founder than others.

In the more backward sects, Lao-tse is the second member of a Holy Trinity. He was born of a virgin mother, who, strangely enough, surpassed all virgin mothers before or since by bringing her son into the world as a full-grown man with long white hair, able to speak the Chinese language and otherwise fully educated.

Most of these sects have more than three gods — they have added a god of war, a god of letters, a god of riches, and a multitude of spirits of whom they live in constant fear. There is a kitchen god who sits always in a prominent corner, observing what goes on in every family, and once a year he makes a trip to heaven to report on what has been going on, both the good and the evil.

Modern Taoism, however, is not entirely devoid of intelligent and ethically minded adherents. There are Taoists who sincerely strive to live up to the exalted philosophy of Lao-tse, and their voice we may well believe is likely to be a more effective factor in the new China that is now rising than ever before.

Let us turn from the religion about Lao-tse to a consideration of the teaching of the philosopher himself, and see what kind of man he was and whether he has anything of importance to say to us in the twentieth century.

He was born in one of the northern kingdoms of China about the year 600 B.C., that middle third of the millennium before the Christian era which witnessed the birth of so many men of spiritual genius in several widely separated areas of the earth, such as the great Hebrew prophets, Amos, Hosea and Isaiah in Palestine; Socrates, Plato and Aristotle in Greece; Buddha and King Asoka in India; Zoroaster in Persia; and Confucius, Mo Ti and Lao-tse in China.

As we have already observed, Lao-tse was an older contemporary of Confucius by forty years or more. It is definitely known that the two men met at least once. Confucius had heard a great deal about Lao-tse and visited him to learn about his philosophy directly from the Master's own lips. He confesses, however, that he was utterly unable to understand it:

I know how birds can fly, fishes swim, and animals run. But the runner may be snared, the swimmer hooked, and the flyer shot by the arrow. But there is the dragon; I cannot tell how he mounts on the wind through the clouds, and rises to heaven. Today I have seen Lao-tse, and can only compare him to the Dragon.[1]

We shall attempt to explain the dragon. We shall attempt to make clear what Confucius confessed his inability to under-

stand. Fortunately, we have before us something to help us
which Confucius did not have, viz., the Tao-Te-King or Book
of the Heavenly Way, which was not written by Lao-tse until
some time after the interview described by Confucius, and
which interview conceivably may have inspired Lao-tse to
work a little harder on making his philosophy more intelligible. As a matter of fact, Lao-tse wrote nothing down on
paper until he was past ninety years of age. And he did so
only when he was close to death and had determined to wander off into a mountain wilderness, there to die in solitary
retreat from civilization.

When a humble tollgate keeper at the bridge that led to
the mountain wilderness persuaded the great philosopher to
put his philosophy down in writing, Lao-tse was most reluctant to do so, but finally yielded to the humble man's
petition, and the result is the prose poem entitled Tao-Te-
King, or the Book of the Heavenly Way, about half the size
of the Gospel of Mark, which can be read in one sitting.

Why was he reluctant to put his thoughts down in writing?
We are not told. Perhaps he was too old and weary, and the
task required a concentration of mind which he was loath
to undertake. Or, perhaps, having been the Court Librarian
for so long and dealing in books as a career, he was anxious
to get away from anything that reminded him of his former
labors. More likely, however, the idea of leaving a book
behind was not wholly consistent with his own philosophy
of life, which had stressed the importance of free and un-
hampered spontaneous living. He believed that writing
things down was an unnatural activity. Man got no pleasure
out of writing. He seems to have agreed with the author of
Ecclesiastes when he wrote, "Of the making of many books
there is no end; and much study is a weariness of the flesh."

He had no ambition to reform the world. He felt that
the world would be much better off if reformers left it alone
and let people alone. The world was suffering from alto-

gether too much civilization, too much improvement in the wrong direction. It was becoming too artificial and too heavy with an excess of so-called wisdom and knowledge.

His was a philosophy of "back to nature," back to the innocent enjoyment of the sun and the moon and the stars and the flowers of the field and birds of the air and beasts of the forest. After his confining hours in the court library he used to go out and commune with nature, not to study it for any use he could make of it later, but for the sheer joy and pleasure of it.

Like Henry Thoreau, who seldom ventured outside the township of his beloved Concord, but "traveled extensively" within the limits of that township, so Lao-tse traveled extensively throughout the community in which he was born. He looked upon people who thought they had to go far afield to find scenes to fill them with wonder as deficient in imagination and common sense.

Like Gandhi, he had no confidence in the multiplicity of the gadgets of civilization contributing to one's inner peace and blessedness. He wanted to get back to the simpler ways of living and of doing things. Like Rousseau, he believed that there was a Natural Law which, if followed, would make life less difficult and complex.

In a small state with a few inhabitants, I would so order it that the people, though supplied with all kinds of implements, would not [care to] use them. . . . Though they had boats and carriages, they should have no occasion to ride in them. Though they had buff-coats and sharp weapons, they should not don them or use them. . . . They should think their coarse food sweet, their plain clothing beautiful, their poor houses places of rest, and their common simple ways sources of enjoyment.[2]

Again,

All things [in nature] spring up without a word spoken, and grow without a claim for their production. They go through their processes without any display of pride in them; and the results are realized without any assumption of ownership. It is owing to the absence of such assumption that the results and their processes do not disappear.[3]

That is to say, it only needs the same quality in the arrangements and measures of government to make human society beautiful and happy.

Lao-tse apparently subscribed to the Jeffersonian doctrine that the least governed people are the best governed:

When the government is blunt and inactive the people will be happy and prosperous;
When the government is discriminative, the people will be dissatisfied and restless. . . .
Who then can know the supremacy [good government]?
Only when the government does no rectifying.[4]

If a ruler has difficulties in governing the people, it is because he trusts too much in material things.

Like all the great seers, Lao-tse taught that material possessions do not produce happiness, that the wise person is he who cultivates the inner life of the mind and character. As Jesus said, "The Kingdom of Heaven is within you," so Lao-tse said:

A master indeed is he whose life activities are from within.
He excels all men.
The sage always teaches the people to know the Inner Life; to desire the Inner Life.
By the practice of Inner Life stillness, we can continually conquer all things. . . .
The wise man dwells in the Inner Life.
He teaches not by words but by actions.[5]

Again,

The sage is not ostentatious, and therefore he shines.
He is not vain, and therefore he is esteemed.
He is not haughty, and therefore he is honored.
The sage teaches without verbosity, he acts without effect, he produces without possessing, he brings his work to perfection

without assuming credit, and claiming nothing as his own, he cannot at any time be said to lose. . . .

To bring forth and preserve, to act without hope of reward, and to expand without waste, this is the supreme virtue.[6]

To create something, to invent a machine, to make a chair, to paint a picture, to find one's joy in one's work, and not in its rewards — this is wisdom.

Like Jesus, he preached the doctrine of returning good for evil.

To those who are good, I act with goodness; to those who are bad, I also act with goodness; thus all get to be good. To those who are sincere, I am sincere; to those who are not sincere I also am sincere; thus all get to be sincere.

The wise man lives in the world in concord and rules over the world in simplicity, he has no self to call his own; he makes the self of the people his self.[7]

Again, like Jesus he preached that the meek shall inherit the earth:

Of the soft and weak things in the world
None is weaker than water;
But in overcoming that which is firm and strong
Nothing can equal it.

That which is weak conquers the strong.
That which is soft conquers the hard. . . .

In life man is soft and tender,
In death he is rigid and hard.
In life plants are soft and pliant,
In death they are withered and tough.
Thus rigidity and hardness are companions of death:
Softness and tenderness are companions of life.[8]

As a philosopher speculating on the ultimate nature of things, he gave utterance to some very profound observations. Looking out on the world, he saw a certain duality running through it all — how everything seems to have an opposite (and its meaning is determined by this opposite). A thing is *high* because another thing is *low;* it is *up* because another is *down;* inside, outside; here, there; near, far. There are the opposites of faith and fear; hope and despair; light, darkness; white, black; male, female; yes, no; north pole, south pole; positive, negative; life, death; existence, non-existence; something, nothing.

He believed that these opposites which gave meaning to each other must have a common unity. Non-existence is important because it is in contrast to existence. The two are vitally related. All opposites are vitally related. The unity behind them he called *Tao.*

> There is a thing inherent and natural,
> Which existed before heaven and earth.
> Motionless and fathomless,
> It stands alone and never changes;
> It pervades everywhere and never becomes exhausted.
> It may be regarded as the Mother of the Universe.
> I do not know its name.
> If I am forced to give it a name,
> I call it Tao, and I name it as supreme.
> Supreme means going on;
> Going on means going far;
> Going far means returning.
> Therefore Tao is supreme. . . .
> Man follows the laws of earth;
> Earth follows the laws of heaven;
> Heaven follows the laws of Tao;
> Tao follows the laws of its intrinsic nature.[9]

The pervasiveness of the Tao is also a characteristic doctrine:

The great Tao pervades everywhere, both on the left and on the right.
By it all things came into being, and it does not reject them.
Merits accomplished, it does not possess them.
It loves and nourishes all things but does not dominate over them.[10]

Very interestingly, an equalitarian conception is added to the pervasiveness of the Tao:

The Tao of heaven brings down that which is high and raises up that which is low. It takes away where there is excess and gives where there is deficiency. The Tao of heaven makes all things equal.[11]

To see life steadily and to see it whole and not become frustrated in any one of its many contradictory aspects — this is to practice Tao.

Whoever develops the Tao in himself will be rooted in virtue; whoever develops the Tao in his family will cause his virtue to spread; whoever develops the Tao in the world will make virtue universal.[12]

Here we have a philosophy that is not far from that of some of our most modern thinkers such as Professor Whitehead and Dr. Einstein.

It seems to me that a people who could produce such thinkers as Lao-tse, Confucius, and Mo Ti, twenty-five centuries ago, and lay the foundations of a civilization that has seen the rise and fall of so many other civilizations, continuing down to our own day with undiminished vitality — surely this people is not to be lightly ignored or treated with anything less than our highest esteem. May we suspect that we may have fully as much to learn from them as we confidently believe that they have much to learn from us.

Surely in their greatest spiritual exemplars and in our own, we can find a large common denominator of ethical insight and philosophical wisdom to constitute a substantial basis for mutual understanding and closer cooperation.

We are so much more like them than unlike them that we have every reason to believe that we can make a success of living together in one world.

When the Ta-Tao or Grand Way prevails, the world is for the welfare of all. Officers are selected because of their virtue and competence. Mutual confidence is promoted and peaceful relations are maintained. People regard not only their own parents as parents, nor only their own children as children. Provisions are made for the aged, employment is provided for the able-bodied, and education is afforded to the young. Widows and widowers, orphans and the childless, the deformed and the diseased, are all cared for. Men have their occupations and women have their homes. Surplus goods are not to be wasted: they need not be kept as one's own. Labor is not to be idle: work is not necessarily for self only. Scheming and intrigues are repressed and banditry and rebellion do not arise. As a result, there is no need of shutting the house-gate at night. Such is the Age of Grand Harmony.

4

Akhnaton and the Concept of One God

HYMN TO ATON

Thy dawning is beautiful in the horizon of heaven,
O living Aton, Beginning of Life!
When thou risest in the eastern horizon of heaven,
Thou fillest every land with thy beauty;
For thou art beautiful, great, glittering, high over the
    earth;

. . . .

How manifold are all thy works!
They are hidden from before us,
O thou sole God, whose powers no other possesseth.
Thou didst create the earth according to thy desire,
While thou wast alone:
Men, all cattle large and small,
All that are upon the earth,
That go upon their feet;
All that are high,
That fly with their wings.

. . . .

How excellent are thy designs, O Lord of eternity!

— AKHNATON

EIGHT CENTURIES BEFORE the time of Confucius, Lao-tse and
Mo Ti, there ruled in Egypt a youthful monarch, who was so
revolutionary in his religious teachings, so sublime in his

ethics, and so daring in his originality that he deserves to rank among the spiritual immortals of the human race.

In point of time, we may regard him as the first great religious genius of whom we have an authentic record.

A few years ago, the name of Akhnaton was scarcely more than a name. But today this name is rich in spiritual meaning and content thanks to the discoveries of modern archeology.

We are more certain today about the earthly existence of Akhnaton and what he actually believed and taught than we are of most of the religious teachers of history.

In the first place, we are in possession of his mummified body, discovered in 1907. We also have a death mask of his face and several pictures and statues of his likeness, made while he was still alive.

In the second place, we have the original letters, hymns and inscriptions he composed.

The oldest manuscript of the New Testament which we possess today was written in the 4th Century A.D. The oldest complete Hebrew manuscript of the Old Testament goes back only to the 9th Century A.D., although since the close of World War II, a copy of the book of Isaiah and one or two others in Hebrew have been discovered which go back to the first or second century before the Christian era.

The teachings of Confucius, Buddha and Zoroaster have come to us by such long roundabout ways, being copies of copies, that their authenticity has been seriously questioned and perhaps will never cease to be questioned. In the case of Akhnaton, however, all doubts have been removed. We are certain not only that we have his body because his name has been inscribed several times on the golden winding sheets that encase it, but also that we have his writings in the original form in which he composed them, on clay tablets discovered at Tell-el-Amarna and on inscriptions to be found on his tomb and his palaces.

Akhnaton was born about 1388 B.C., in the ancient city of Thebes. He was the only son of Amenhotep III. When he was born, he was not called Akhnaton, but Amenhotep IV. This was the name he used until he was seventeen years of age.

Proud Pharaohs who claimed their descent from the gods were accustomed to include the name of their favorite deity in the name they gave their children.

Amon was the favorite deity of Thebes at that time as well as the Chief God among all Egyptian divinities, and there were a great number. The priesthood of Amon was very powerful. The cult of Amon was very popular. Hence the son of the Pharaoh was called Amenhotep, meaning the Peace of Amon. He was a sickly boy — without doubt an epileptic. He had a large, elongated head and a protruding chin, but a delicately moulded mouth. He was a quiet, studious and precocious child, very fond of taking long walks by himself. Before he was eleven years of age, he was married to the daughter of a Syrian King, a princess by the name of Nofretete. Soon after he was eleven, his father died and the young Pharaoh ascended to the throne.

His mother, Queen Tiy, assumed the real leadership of the empire until Amenhotep became of age at sixteen. Then things began to happen.

The new Pharaoh decided to overhaul the religion of his ancestors. He decided to repudiate the cult of Amon and all the other religious cults of Egypt. One day he suddenly announced that there was only one true God, namely Aton, who was the source of all life and energy, the Father of all men and nations, the Creator of Earth and Heaven, the Master of all Fate.

Aton was symbolized by the sun's disk. Aton was to be worshipped in spirit and in truth.

The first step of this reformation was to wipe out all traces of the cult of Amon which, of course, resulted merely in that cult being driven underground. Akhnaton's next step was to build a new city to the honor of this new God. Thebes was a constant reminder of Amon and the Amon priesthood. Accordingly, he sailed down the Nile to a spot about one hundred and fifty miles south of the present Cairo and there, where the high cliffs on the east bank of the Nile recede to form a semi-circle about an enclosed plain, he decided to build the physical foundation of his new faith. Thus, "The Horizon of Aton," as it was called — came into existence. It was a beautiful city — magnificently laid out with a high temple to the new God and several palaces for the King and his royal ministers. The major portion of Egypt's resources went into the building of this city, in beautifying its streets and parks and enriching its cultural life. There Akhnaton moved his capital when he was nineteen years of age. There he lived the rest of his life. There he died and was buried. There in the rock cliffs surrounding his beloved city can be found his tomb today.

This man has been called the first individual of History. Whether this be deserved or not, he certainly stands out from all the other Pharaohs of Egypt. He was something different.

He was the first heretic. He broke completely with the religion of his time. There was scarcely anything in his new faith that could be found in the old. The changes which he effected were nothing short of revolutionary. They were so revolutionary, in fact, that the common people could not comprehend what it was all about. Akhnaton, of course, made some genuine converts to his heresy — but it ever remained a heresy. He incurred the undying hatred of the Amon priesthood and the priesthood of all other cults. If he had been anyone but a Pharaoh, his life would have been forfeited without question. As Pharaoh, it was possible for him to play the role of heretic and still remain alive. He was one of the few heretics in religion with the distinction of having been tolerated instead of persecuted.

He was the first monotheist of which we have any record. The God of Moses was a tribal deity. The God of Elijah was a great God above the other gods. But the God of Akhnaton was the one and only God — without rivals or near rivals of any kind.

Aton was the Formless Essence, the Intelligent Germ, the Loving Force that permeated time and space. He was symbolized by the Sun and especially manifest in the rays of the sun, but he was not to be identified with the sun. He was the energy behind the sun, the creator of the sun and the moon and the stars, the ultimate source of light and heat, the primal motive power of all living things. No graven image of Aton was permitted. The true God had no form. No one was to attempt any pictorial representation of him or be found worshipping any such representation.

Aton was not a Lord of Hosts, like Jehovah, but a Lord of Peace. Human bloodshed in war or in religious sacrifices was abhorrent to him. He was not to be found in the confusion of battles or in the smoke of sacrifices but in the beauty of the flowers and the trees and the wild ducks flying and fishes playing and clouds passing by. He was not a God of Wrath, but a God of Forgiveness who took no pleasure in vengeance, jealousy or cruelty, who desired the universal salvation and happiness of his children.

He was a God of Love, "who heareth the sobs of the hungry infant and the bleatings of the lost lamb and even listeneth when the chicken crieth in the egg shell."

"O Aton Thou fillest the two lands of Egypt with thy love. Thy love is great and large. Thy rays encompass the lands. Thou bindest them with love," declares one of his Psalms.

Aton was a God of Truth. "Living in Truth," was his other name. "I have set truth in my inward parts and falsehood is my loathing," saith the Lord. "They that worship me must worship me in truth."

He was a God of Joy who took delight in the happiness of all life.

"He made the lambs to dance upon thin legs and the birds to flutter in the marshes."

He was to be worshipped best by joyous living at all times of the day, but especially during the hours of sunrise and sunset when the beauty of Aton's glory was at its height.

How sublime, how transcendent, how holy and ethical was Akhnaton's God!

Purified of all superstitions and crudities that attach to most of the gods of antiquity, Aton compares favorably with the Heavenly Father of Jesus and with the God of the most recent philosophers such as Whitehead and Eddington.

Akhnaton was a thorough-going monotheist, a thousand years before the word was even coined. He was the first preacher of universal salvation. In his conception of the after-life, there was no hell, no place of torment, no devouring monsters, no lake of fire and brimstone.

According to the beliefs of his time, the soul at death must pass through awful places to the judgment throne of Osiris where it was weighed in the balances. There were so many spirits and demons on the way which must be placated by a ritual of incantations — the correct repetition of which alone assured safe passage — that the average individual in Egypt at that time was constantly in fear of the terrors of the after-life.

Akhnaton thrust all these teachings aside. He insisted that when a man died, his soul took on an immaterial body and went directly to Heaven, which was bathed in eternal sunshine and cooled by the breath of the north wind and perfumed by the scent of thyme. Sometimes this soul visited the earth to see if its name was held in remembrance, otherwise it took no interest in earthly events, but revelled in the joys of Heaven.

Akhnaton was the first apostle of the simple life. He wore

no jewelry. He drove through the city streets unaccompanied
by a retinue of soldiers. He took delight in innocent amusements. He ate simple fare but he was far from being an
ascetic. He drank of the flowing bowl and loved the sound
of beautiful music. He lived close to nature.

He lived close to his family. He was not ashamed to be
seen caressing his wife or playing with his children. He had
seven daughters but no son. It is seldom that this Pharaoh
is pictured without his family. He called his wife "Mother
of My Happiness." Even on the most ceremonious occasions,
the queen sat beside her husband and held his hand while
their children frolicked about them. In opposition to all
custom, he ordered that his queen be shown upon the same
scale of size and importance as that of himself. He laid great
stress upon the sanctity of marriage and the duties of parent-
hood. He wanted his private life to be an example to his
people, just as did Marcus Aurelius, centuries later.

It is true that as Pharaoh he received much homage and
that he still retained the idea of his divine right to rule, but
through it all, he never lost sight of the fact that he was
primarily a man. He was about as democratic in his ways
as it was possible for a Pharaoh to be and remain a Pharaoh.

He ordered that all sculptors and painters portray him
exactly as he looked, with all his physical defects and peculiarities. They obliged him accordingly. The impetus
which he gave to realism in this respect brought about the
greatest Renaissance in art that Egypt had ever had. It
reached a height of perfection that was only surpassed by
the art of Greece. It was characterized by the beauty and
naturalness of simplicity. The two great artists of that period,
Bek and Aut, claimed that the young Pharaoh had taught
them all that they knew, and had been their chief inspiration.

Akhnaton was the first prophet of peace through non-
resistance. He believed that Aton abhorred war and he had
the courage to stand by his convictions. When the Hittites

began to threaten the security of his far-flung empire, his vassals, the kings of Syria and Babylon, sent hurried dispatches to the Pharaoh begging for Egyptian armies to defend their cities, but the help they asked for did not come. It never came while Akhnaton was alive. They were asking an uncompromising idealist to deny his faith in his own ideals. Bit by bit his empire began to fall to pieces. Letter after letter came, asking him for help. Still the Pharaoh refused to take the sword. He finally paid the penalty for this refusal by living to see the great power which he had inherited from his father reduced to a mere fragment of what it had once been.

It is easy to see why Akhnaton's reign was brief and why he came to an untimely death before he was yet thirty years of age. He was trying to live a religion that was thousands of years ahead of his age, and the immensity of the task was too much for his frail constitution. He was essentially a prophet. He had no business being a king. He was a round peg in a square hole, a poet compelled to play the role of a politician, a mystic become monarch, and a Jesus in the seat of Pilate.

When he sang in his hymn to Aton,

> The countries of Syria and Nubia,
> The land of Egypt,
> Thou settest every man in his place,
> Thou suppliest their necessities,[1]

he was proclaiming the Fatherhood of God and the Brotherhood of Man. He was not helping very much to protect his own far-flung empire.

And yet, proclaiming the Fatherhood of God and the Brotherhood of Man may have been the more important task. Who knows? Perhaps when this idea which was planted by Akhnaton becomes fully grown, it will protect empires far better than they have ever been protected in the past. At any rate, here was a sublime heretic who had the courage to practice his heresy as well as preach it.

As one of his modern biographers has so ably said:

He has given us an example three thousand years ago which might be followed at the present day: an example of what a husband and a father should be, of what an honest man should do, of what a poet should feel, of what a preacher should teach, of what an artist should strive for, of what a scientist should believe, of what a philosopher should think. Like other great teachers he sacrificed all to his principles, and thus his life plainly shows — alas! — the impracticability of his doctrines; yet there can be no question that his ideals will hold good "till the swan turns black and the crow turns white, till the hills rise up to travel, and the deeps rush into the rivers." [2]

5

Krishna and the Law of Compensation

Neither a man who lives unrighteously
  Nor he who acquires wealth by telling falsehoods,
Nor he who always delights in doing injury,
  Ever attains happiness in this world.
. . . .
But an iniquity, once committed, never fails
  To produce fruit to him who wrought it.
He prospers for a while through unrighteousness;
  Then he gains great good fortune;
Next he conquers his enemies;
  But at last he perishes, branch and root.

— LAWS OF MANU

LET US CONSIDER the religion of Hinduism with special reference to the mythical personality whom the Hindus call the "Blessed Lord Krishna."

The Lord Krishna is not to be understood as the real or alleged founder of Hinduism, for the religion of Hinduism had no founder. Its origins are lost in the haze of a remote and hoary antiquity. Some of the sacred books of this religion extend back forty to fifty centuries. The Vedic hymns, for instance, antedate the oldest portion of our Bible, not by centuries, but by at least two millenniums. In the course of its development, Hinduism both descended far below its lofty beginnings, accumulating so many gods in the process

42

that it would take hours just to mention their names. At the same time, it forged above that level in other respects, especially in its profound discernment of spiritual and ethical principles, so that today we have a vast system of conglomerate beliefs, puzzling incongruities and irreconcilable contradictions, which defy the comprehension of any man.

Someone has said that one could spend a lifetime in the serious study of this religion and at the end be able to touch merely the hem of its garment. It has about one hundred thousand temples, wayside shrines and holy places, but it has no organized church as such, and it never has had a Pope.

James Freeman Clarke has said in substance that Hinduism has a philosophy as brilliant, profound and spiritual as any in the world, yet it is weighted down with gross superstitions, and cruel practices. It has a belief so abstract that it almost escapes the grasp of the most speculative intellect, but at the same time, it is joined to the notion that sin can be atoned for by bathing in the Ganges River, or reciting a verse from one of the Vedic hymns. It teaches that it is not religious to kill a worm, or even tread upon a single blade of grass and yet some of its adherents have been guilty of tortures and cruelties which would shock a Nero or a Borgia. Half the best informed writers in India will tell you that Hinduism is a religion of pure monotheism; the other half will just as promptly assert that it worships a million gods; some that it is the profoundest philosophy of life ever conceived by man, others that its idolatry is more gross than that of any living people.[1]

If this be so, you can see how utterly presumptuous it is for anyone even to attempt to give a true picture of this religion in one short chapter. Let us therefore concentrate on merely one phase of what is obviously good in Hinduism, namely, the Song of the Lord Krishna, as we find it in the Bhagavad-Gita, which is to the people in India what the Jewish Book of Psalms is to us in America. Portions of the

Bhagavad-Gita were read daily by the late Mahatma Gandhi. He also read from the Vedas, the Upanishads, the Laws of Manu and the Mahabharata of which the Bhagavad-Gita is a part. But it was the last which constituted his greatest inspiration, as it is today the inspiration of Pandit Nehru, the distinguished Prime Minister of India.

Historical research cannot precisely date the origin of the Bhagavad-Gita. It was probably composed before the beginning of our era.[2] Although the Bhagavad-Gita is almost wholly an account of the speeches of the Lord Krishna, they were not composed or uttered by him but by some unknown poet who put his own words into the mouth of India's most popular divinity.

For the Lord Krishna is a mythical creation of the religious imagination. He never lived as an historical personality any more than Apollo, Venus, Mithra or Mars. He was not like Confucius, Lao-tse or Gautama, or Jesus, who were real human beings about whom legends grew up until the process of idealization had transformed them into deities. But like Apollo, Venus, Mithra and Mars, he began as a God and was only afterward clothed with the attributes of human personality and given an earthly biography. Herein is one of the legitimate distinctions between a legend and a myth, whether in reference to an event or a personality. A legend is a fact dressed up in fiction, a myth is a fiction dressed up in the semblance of fact. In both cases, the purpose is to convey a truth or what is conceived to be a truth. The Lord Krishna was a mythical personality, who was later given a human biography. He was represented as the son of a King, saved from the slaughter of the innocents, brought up by a cowherd, making sport with the milkmaids in his childhood, and performing many miraculous feats for their amusement and delight.

When he becomes of age, he marries the daughter of a king, and her image is often seen, together with his, in India's temples today. Among his many names he is called "the Lord of the Milkmaids" and also "The Good Cowherd," which is, of course, comparable to our designation of Jesus as "the Good Shepherd," for it has the same connotations of devoutness and reverence.

That you may judge for yourselves, the mythical character of the Lord Krishna, let us turn directly to the Bhagavad-Gita where he says of himself:

I [am] the Father of this universe, the Mother, the Supporter, the Grandsire, the Holy One to be known, the Word of Power . . . the Path, Husband, Lord, Witness, Abode, Shelter, Lover, Origin, Dissolution, Foundation, Treasure-house, Seed imperishable. I give heat; I hold back and send forth the rain; immortality and also death, being and non-being am I. . . . Earth, water, fire, air, ether, Mind, and Reason also and Egoism — these are the eightfold divisions of My nature. . . . I am the source of the forthgoing of the whole universe and likewise the place of its dissolving. . . . I [am] . . . the radiance in moon and sun; the Word of Power in all the Vedas, sound in ether, and virility in men; the pure fragrance of earths and the brilliance in fire am I. . . . I am the Reason of the Reason-endowed, the splendour of splendid things am I. . . . All beings have root in me, I am not rooted in them. . . . He who offereth to Me with devotion a leaf, a flower, a fruit, water, that I accept from the striving self, offered as it is with devotion. . . . They verily who worship Me with devotion, they are in me, and I also in them. Even if the most sinful worship Me, with undivided heart, he too must be accounted righteous.[3]

Surely it is evident that here we have one clothed with the attributes of deity, not a flesh and blood human being speaking. When someone called Jesus "Good Master," Jesus replied, "Why callest thou me good? none is good, save one, even God." Jesus never identified himself with God, at least not in the first three Gospels. It is only in the less authentic Gospel of John (to which historical research assigns a second century date) that Jesus speaks after the manner of the Lord Krishna, and arrogates to himself attributes of divinity.

The Krishna of the Bhagavad-Gita and the Christ of the Fourth Gospel have very much in common; both are august and holy figures; both speak of an exalted way of life. "Know the truth and the truth shall make you free," says the Lord Christ in the Gospel of John. The Lord Krishna in the Bhagavad-Gita says, "Knowing the truth, thy heart no more will ache with error for the truth shall show all things subdued to thee as thou art to me. There is no purifier like thereto in all this world, and he who seeketh truth shall find it and grow perfect in himself."

What does it mean to know the truth? What is the truth? According to Krishna it is to know that man

> . . . is not born, nor doth he die; nor having been, ceaseth he any more to be; unborn, perpetual, eternal and ancient, he is not slain when the body is slaughtered. . . . As a man, casting off worn-out garments, taketh new ones, so the dweller in the body, casting off worn-out bodies, entereth into others that are new. Weapons cleave him not, nor fire burneth him, nor waters wet him, nor wind drieth him away. . . . For certain is death for the born, and certain is birth for the dead; therefore over the inevitable thou shouldst not grieve.[4]

Here we have clearly enunciated the doctrine of reincarnation, which runs through all forms of the Hindu faith. This was not the first formulation of this doctrine by any means — hints of it can be found in the more ancient Vedic hymns. Hindu philosophy sees no difference in kind, but only in degree, between the life of man and that of the animal and vegetable world. It preached the doctrine of evolution ages before Darwin appeared, but it preached an evolution of the spirit as well as that of the human body.

As the human body has developed from lowly physical forms, so the human personality has undergone a corresponding spiritual evolution through countless former incarnations — the events and experiences of which have been lost to the conscious memory, but the results of which are stored up as skills and spiritual capacities in the deep recesses of the human soul.

The Hindu faith contends that what can be created can be destroyed, but the soul, never having been created, cannot be destroyed.

This doctrine of reincarnation is, of course, one of those speculations of the human mind which can neither be proved nor disproved. But surely it is just as plausible as the speculation which holds that the soul of man did have a beginning in time but will have no end, or that it never did exist and does not exist now, except as a result of physical forces, like a flame kindled when we strike a match, but which goes out with the blowing of the wind.

Probably more people in the world believe in the doctrine of reincarnation than in any other, but, of course, that does not make it so.

Closely associated with this teaching is the doctrine of Karma, which is taken for granted by the author of the Bhagavad-Gita. The doctrine of Karma has frequently been misrepresented by western critics of Hinduism as being identical with fatalism. But this is not the case. Fatalism leaves no room for freedom of the human will. It signifies that everything that happened to us was preordained from the very beginning and we can do nothing to change it; that, whatever we get in life, be it pain or pleasure, joy or sorrow, triumph or defeat, was determined long before we were born, and when the time has come for us to die, nothing can be done to hasten or postpone the event.

The doctrine of Karma, however, does make room for the freedom of the human will; it is more like Emerson's law of compensation, which states: "We are punished by our sins — not for them," or again, like Paul's teaching that "whatsoever a man soweth, that also shall he reap." The teaching implied in the Law of Karma may be summarized in these words: We cannot escape the consequences of the evil we have done or fail to reap the benefits of the good we have achieved. If a man sows tares, he will reap tares, but if he sows wheat, he will reap wheat. He is free to sow either and under compulsion to sow neither, but whatever he does or does not sow, he is not free from its consequences. If he tells lies, sooner or later those lies will exact their penalties in his not being trusted in some crucial emergency when he is telling the truth and needs to be believed. By the same token, a life of selfishness and greed, of lust and sensuality, will bring its own punishments in the loss of spiritual awareness. There is a moral law undergirding the universe that even the gods cannot break without breaking themselves upon it. If you do not learn this lesson in one lifetime, you will have to come back in another incarnation and try once more. You cannot move up to the next grade in the school of life which this universe keeps until you have passed the requirements of the grade in which you find yourself. Everyone comes into life at the level he formerly left off and whether he reaches the higher level and how fast is entirely up to his own efforts.

Some people are born into this world with an obvious heritage of spiritual wisdom while others seem to be bogged down by primitive appetites and impulses. This disparity in native endowment was not decreed by the gods, but by the choices and desires of these very people in a former existence.

Ancient Hinduism did not recognize the part played by fortunate or unfortunate environment in fashioning the desire of the soul. Modern Hinduism, however, does. A man like Pandit Nehru is interested in lifting the people in India out of their present poverty and misery not only as a means of expressing the good impulses of his own spirit, but because of the influence that a more propitious environment will have upon the inner spiritual life of the Indian people. The ideal human being as described by the Bhagavad-Gita and put into the mouth of the Lord Krishna, over twenty centuries ago, is still his goal as it is the goal of a host of others who are the spiritual leaders of India today.

And what are the qualities which constitute the ideal human being? The Bhagavad-Gita says:

. . . humbleness,
Uprightness, heed to injure nought which lives;
Truthfulness, slowness unto wrath, a mind
That lightly letteth go what others prize,
Equanimity and charity
Which spieth no man's faults; and tenderness
Towards all that suffer; a contented heart,
Fluttered by no desires; a bearing mild,
Modest and grave; with manhood nobly mixed;
With patience, fortitude, and purity;
An unrevengeful spirit, never given
To rate itself too high — such be the signs
Of him whose feet are set on that fair path which leads to heavenly birth.[5]

Surely this picture of the Hindu ideal does not differ greatly from that of the Christian saint. If a religion is entitled to be judged by its highest achievements, then Hinduism does not compare unfavorably with Christianity — either in the ethical beauty of the character it has inspired, or in the lyrical quality of the literature it has brought forth. If we are to point out the faults and limitations of Hindu life and culture, we must in fairness not overlook our own. It is not just to compare the worst in them with the best in ourselves.

If India has her Untouchables, only recently emancipated by law, let us not forget that we have our second-class citizens, in spite of a proclamation of emancipation made over three-quarters of a century ago. If India has her sacred cows wandering in the streets and treated more or less as pets, we have probably just as many dogs running loose on our streets.

The Hindus do not eat the flesh of cows any more than we use our dogs for food.

If the priestly class in India seems to us to have assumed an overweening role in Hindu life, exerting an influence far beyond what is wholesome for the good of the country as a whole, the Hindu replies by pointing to the enormous hold which our commercial and industrial leaders have upon our western way of life all out of proportion to their number in the body politic. They also point to the dictatorship of the proletariat in Russia as another example of undue power of one class over another. If we accuse them of being polytheistic, pointing to their three chief gods, Brahma, Vishnu and Shiva, and a host of lesser deities, they ask us about our Trinity of Father, Son and Holy Ghost; and also about our Santa Claus, the Grim Reaper, Father Time, Dan Cupid, Jack Frost, the Sandman, not to speak of his Satanic Majesty — all of whom are mythical personalities — to whom we refer partly as a matter of convenience and partly as a matter of polytheistic survival in our culture, but whose names we speak no less seriously than the Hindu often speaks of his various gods and goddesses.

In America death is pictured as a gruesome skeleton but in India as a handsome young man with a comforting smile on his lips. The Hindu says he prefers his myth to ours.

There is a story in the Upanishads, which tells of a disciple asking his Master how many gods there are, and the Master replied, "As many as are mentioned in the Sacred Scriptures — three and three thousand." "Yes," he said, and asked again, "How many gods are there, really, Master?" This time the Master said, "Thirty-three." The persistent disciple repeated his question again and again, the Master each time reducing the number respectively to six, three, two, one and a half, and finally to one. "Yes," said the disciple, who asked, "Who then are these three and three thousand?" The Master replied, "They are only the various manifestations of the one almighty power."[6]

There is no chance of an agreement or understanding between India or America if either is bent on finding fault with the other and is determined to judge the other by its worst features. Every people, every culture, every religion is entitled to be judged by its highest achievements. Using this test, let us ask if Christianity or any other religion in modern times has produced anyone to surpass the late Mahatma Gandhi in undeviating devotion to the truth, in courageous championship of the downtrodden, in broad humanitarian compassion, in deeds of mercy and forgiveness, in sustained self-discipline and self-mastery, in sheer spiritual radiance and moral grandeur or in complete trust in the will of God — and yet Gandhi was a Hindu. This Hindu was generous enough to acknowledge publicly his great debt to the teachings of Jesus by way of Henry Thoreau and Count Leo Tolstoy, but he believed he owed a greater debt to the faith in which he was born and in which he died.

6

Buddha and the Eightfold Path

To dwell in a pleasant land, with right desires in
the heart —
This is the greatest blessing.
Self-control and pleasant speech, and whatever word
be well spoken —
This is the greatest blessing.
To live righteously, to give help to kindred, to
follow a peaceful calling —
This is the greatest blessing.
Beneath the stroke of life's changes, the mind that
shaketh not, without grief or passion, and secure —
This is the greatest blessing.
Let us live happily, free from care among the busy.
Let us dwell free from yearning among men who
are anxious.
Let us live happily, not hating those who hate us.
Let us, therefore, overcome anger by kindness, evil
by good, falsehood by truth.
Let us speak the truth; yield not to anger; give
when asked, even from the little that we have.
By these three things shall we enter the presence of
the gods.

— BUDDHA

BUDDHISM BEGAN IN INDIA and spread rapidly to China,
Tibet, Ceylon and Japan. It is now more popularly supported in these four countries than in the land of its origin.

There are about seven million Buddhists in India today.
But this faith has from three hundred and fifty to five hundred million adherents in the rest of Asia.[1] There are about
two hundred thousand in America. Roughly speaking, one-
fifth to one-fourth of the population of the earth belong to
this faith, and Buddhism, like Islam, Mormonism, Christian

52

Science, and Bahaism, is one of the few religions which were
deliberately founded.

Buddha was its real as well as its alleged founder.

Like many other luminary figures in history, so many
myths and legends have gathered about his name that it is
difficult to recover the historical personality. Yet here are
the facts as near as modern research can untangle them. Siddartha Gautama Sakya Buddha was born in northeastern
India near the foothills of the Himalaya Mountains about
the year 563 B.C.

He was thus a contemporary of Confucius, Lao-tse and
Mo Ti.

Siddartha was his personal name, Gautama his family
name; Sakya was his tribal name and Buddha, which means
"the Enlightened One," was the religious name given to him
by his disciples, just as Jesus of Nazareth was called the
Christ, which means the Anointed One.

Unlike Jesus, however, he was not born in poverty and
obscurity, but like Akhnaton, Isaiah, and King Asoka, he
was born amidst regal splendor and luxury.

Gautama was the son of a wealthy Indian prince. He was
married at the age of nineteen years to a beautiful princess.
She bore him one son.

He was a brilliant, handsome and dashing youth, who,
until he was thirty years of age, revelled unrestrained in
princely luxury, drinking the cup of pleasure in wild abandonment, swiftly passing from one indulgence to another
until his sensitive nature finally grew tired and rebelled.

All of a sudden life seemed to become stale and empty in
spite of its apparent fullness. His soul longed for some satisfying experience which his sheltered existence could not give
him. The misery and degradation of the world about him
troubled his conscience. He could not justify to himself his
palatial luxury in the presence of all this misery. A chance
excursion into this world from which he had been deliber-

ately sheltered opened his eyes to the fact that life must surely mean something more than mere pleasure seeking.

So one night, he decides resolutely to give up his princely pleasures once and for all and seek a new life. Taking a last fond farewell look at his sleeping wife and child, he quietly but quickly leaves the palace under the cover of darkness. Accompanied by a faithful servant he mounts his favorite horse and rides forth into the night and he does not stop until he is completely beyond the boundaries of his father's kingdom.

There he strips himself of his sword and his ornaments and sends his servant back with these and the horse to his father.

Not until he exchanges his clothes with a beggar whom he meets on the way does he feel himself free at last from all associations with his former world. He does not worry about his wife and son. He is confident they will be cared for until the day he returns.

He first joins a school of hermit philosophers who carry on long arguments about metaphysical subjects in a mountain cave, but soon comes to the conclusion that the best philosophy of his day is utterly barren and bankrupt. "Philosophy is merely the pastime of flying kites in the air. It doesn't affect the climate in which men live."

He next decides to join a group of ascetics and spends six years in the Indian jungle, subjecting himself to all kinds of self-inflictions, endeavoring to live on such a restricted diet that he finally becomes a mere shadow of his former physical self. Eventually he reaches the conclusion that pain is just as vain a path to peace of mind as abstract philosophy or pleasure. Instead of thinking less about food, he finds himself thinking about it most of the time.

So he gives up the ascetic life in disgust and despair.

This time he wanders off by himself and takes refuge under a bo tree by a certain river bank and there he spends a day and night in deep and earnest meditation.

And then, when morning dawns a light breaks upon him and there comes to him, like a sudden revelation from Heaven, his vision of the Four Noble Truths and the Eightfold Path.

Gathering about him a company of disciples, he instructs them in the doctrines of his new discovery and sends them forth on a preaching mission to the rest of India.

Eventually he returns to his wife and son. These and the rest of his family are among his first converts.

He spends the whole of his time thereafter in teaching and preaching, his favorite meeting place a deer park in Benares, which has since become one of the world's holiest shrines.

Dying at the ripe old age of eighty years, he leaves to the world the example of a sincere, kindly and wise personality which has been and still is one of the great inspirations of mankind. Probably one person out of every four today — certainly one out of every five — speaks of him as the Blessed Lord Buddha.

What was it that Gautama discovered under the Bo Tree? What were the Four Noble Truths which broke upon him like a brilliant light from heaven? Briefly, they are four observations about life in general.

The first Truth states that the world is full of spiritual suffering and sorrow. It is full of worry, discouragement, disillusionment and discontent. People are never as happy as they think they are going to be. This is just as true of the rich as the poor, of the learned as of the illiterate. Alexander Pope has summed it up:

> Hope springs eternal in the human breast.
> Man never is but always to be blest.

The second Truth is that the cause of this misery is an illusion. Mankind is the victim of the illusion of selfish desire. He allows himself to entertain a multitude of wants and wishes, which can never be fully satisfied in the very nature of things. The more he gets — the more he wants. The fact that most people take their selfish desires seriously is the basic source of all human suffering.

Selfish desire is the arrow in the side of suffering humanity. Remove the arrow and the wound will heal of itself.

Recognize that the source of all man's misery, pain, disappointment, and anguish, lies in his longing for certain selfish gratifications; then progressively extinguish these longings and there will come the cool peace of Nirvana.

Nirvana, or soul serenity, is equal to what a man has, divided by what he wants. If he has something and wants nothing, then one divided by zero makes for infinite peace of mind.

The third Truth is to realize that one can never have true peace of mind by trying to satisfy his selfish wants and wishes, for every time he thinks he has succeeded in satisfying a given want, behold, another rises up to claim its place — and more likely than not, many rise up to claim its place.

No, the path to soul serenity does not lie in increasing the numerator of satisfaction, but in decreasing the denominator of selfish desire. It lies in simplifying one's wants and wishes with the idea of ultimately becoming completely detached from them.

Finally, the way to become detached from self-seeking satisfactions (and herein lies the originality of Buddha) is not the method of direct but indirect attack. It is not to mortify the flesh or to do penance or to fast from food or to take vows of self-renunciation; these methods cannot help at all. They but strengthen the desires by focusing attention upon them. The way to achieve detachment and serenity of soul is rather by the method of a life of positive unselfishness. In short, the way to forget one's desires and anxieties is to lose one's self in devotion to something bigger and higher than the self.

This is essentially the discovery which Jesus made some

five hundred and fifty years afterward, a discovery which is psychologically and sociologically profound.

The Eightfold Path of Buddha is not far from the spirit which animates Christ's Sermon on the Mount. "Whoever shall save his life, shall lose it. Whosoever shall lose his life . . . shall save it."

The first Path is called Right Views.

We have a saying that ignorance of the law is no excuse. By the same token, Buddha held that there is such a thing as culpable ignorance of the truth.

The first loyalty of those who would attain soul serenity is loyalty to the whole truth and nothing but the truth regardless of consequences.

To be superstitious and ignorant is to be guilty of self-indulgence. Everyone is under obligation to exert himself to know as much of the truth as possible.

The second Path is called Right Ambitions.

Fame, power, pride of social status, one's own personal happiness and welfare are not right ambitions because they cannot reasonably be fulfilled in this life, but the ambition to serve the welfare of others is a legitimate one, for failure here, or limited success, does not result in feelings of frustration and defeat.

The third and fourth Paths are called Right Utterance and Right Conduct.

One's words and actions should be kindly, truthful and helpful without obtrusiveness or egotism. The three famous monkeys: Hear no Evil, Speak no Evil, and See no Evil, are Buddhist in origin, adorning the Buddhist Temple of Nikko in Japan.

The fifth Path is called Right Livelihood.

One must choose only those means of obtaining a living which are free from the deception or exploitation of one's fellow men. No one can obtain real peace of mind who lives by taking advantage of other human beings. He will always be on his guard lest the one exploited may rise up against him sooner or later.

The sixth Path is called Right Effort.

There is no salvation in good intentions by themselves. Good intentions must find expression in earnest endeavor or they are no good at all.

The seventh Path is called Right Motives.

The disciple is to beware lest he find himself even doing unselfish deeds for the sake of praise and appreciation. No one can attain to soul serenity if he is conscious of what impression he is making on others.

He who looks for the smallest grain of gratitude will never reach it.

The most disillusioned people in the world are those who demand gratitude from others and expect to get it. Life simply does not respond in this way.

The eighth Path is called Right Meditation.

The disciple is not to petition the gods for anything for himself — not even the blessing of soul serenity.

One should pray neither for personal survival after death on the one hand, nor for complete oblivion on the other; but one should learn to look upon both with such detachment that the thought of either fate becomes a matter of equal indifference. Infinite truth, infinite justice, infinite mercy — these are the only objectives worthy of serious meditation. This, in short, is the Gospel of Buddhism. What a pity that it should have been allowed to languish in the land of its birth!

Under King Asoka, who became a convert a century after the death of Buddha, it once became the principal faith of India and created the nearest approach to a Kingdom of Heaven on earth that this world has ever seen, according to H. G. Wells. But after King Asoka, Buddhism was gradually absorbed by Hinduism and lost its identity except for the seven million adherents of today.

What a greater pity that such a simple gospel in spreading to Tibet, China, Burma and Japan, should have become so corrupted in its pilgrimage as to make room for prayer wheels, superstitious ceremonies, magical sacraments and a highly organized priesthood. Buddha in the course of time was given a virgin for a mother. Many miracles were attributed to him such as turning water into wine and feeding the multitudes with a few loaves and fishes. His disciples were believed to have walked upon the sea. Buddha himself became the third member of a Holy Trinity. His church divided into two main groups and numerous sects.

Even so, in modern Buddhism, as far removed as it is from the simplicity of its founder, there are still three important universal values which the rest of the world cannot afford to neglect.

First, the sacredness of all life; even the snail and the bamboo-sprout have a life that should not be carelessly wasted.

Second, the importance of tolerance. Buddha did not claim to have the whole truth and nothing but the truth. He is reported as having said, "There were Buddhas before me and there are greater ones to come. I was not the first, nor shall I be the last." Buddhism has had no general inquisition, no heresy trials and no holy wars, except possibly one in Tibet, a long time ago. No true Buddhist today can be obsessed with the idea that he has the whole truth. Therefore, he is eclectic — many a Buddhist being also a Taoist, a Confucianist, or a Christian, in addition.

The third important contribution is its emphasis on the value of man's inner life.

The test of a successful career among Buddhists is not how much wealth one has accumulated nor how much fame he has won, nor how much power he can wield, nor how much learning he has acquired; but rather, how much good he has achieved, how many things he has learned to do without, from how many enslaving illusions, passions, prejudices and ambitions has he freed himself. What is the condition of his mind? What is the state of his soul?

If he has no peace of mind, no sense of self-mastery, if his spirit is distracted and disturbed by fears, jealousies, restless ambitions, vain regrets about the past and foolish anxieties about the future, then no matter how successful outwardly he may appear to be, he has made a miserable failure of his life.

The Buddhist ideal is one who has realistically rejected all desires that can never be satisfied, and cultivated only those desires that offer some hope of fulfillment. Henry Wotton has described this ideal as well as anyone:

> How happy is he born or taught
>   Who serveth not another's will;
> Whose armor is his honest thought,
>   And simple truth his highest skill;
>
> Whose passions not his masters are;
>   Whose soul is still prepared for death,
> Untied unto the world by care
>   Of prince's ear or vulgar breath;
>
> Who hath his life from rumors freed,
>   Whose conscience is his strong retreat,
> Whose state can neither flatterers feed,
>   Nor ruin make oppressors great;
>
> Who God doth late and early pray
>   More of his grace than goods to lend;
> And walks with man, from day to day,
>   As with a brother and a friend.
>
> This man is freed from servile bands
>   Of hope to rise, or fear to fall;
> Lord of himself, though not of lands,
>   And having nothing, yet hath all.

Here we have the Buddhist way of life — a life of dignity, compassion and deep inward poise and peace.

7

King Asoka and the Rock Edicts

Amidst the tens of thousands of names of monarchs that crowd the columns of history, their majesties and graciousnesses and serenities and royal highnesses and the like, the name of Asoka shines, and shines almost alone, a star. From the Volga to Japan his name is still honored. China, Tibet and even India, though it has left his doctrine, preserve the tradition of his greatness. More living men cherish his memory to-day than have ever heard the names of Constantine or Charlemagne.

— H. G. WELLS

KING ASOKA, THE BUDDHIST KING of ancient India, is to be numbered among the great saints of history.

To some, a saint is a pale, anemic, emaciated being who is ready, yes, even anxious, to quit "this vale of tears and sordidness" for some other and more holy clime, and only condescends to remain here on earth because of an uncomfortable sense of duty.

To others, a saint is a heretic long since dead — dead at least a hundred years — who was first "enthusiastically cannonaded before he was ecclesiastically canonized."

Neither definition is adequate. In my judgment, a saint is one who possesses a quickened conscience, who strenuously strives to lift his life to the level of that conscience and attains to such a measure of success that his example is a powerful source of inspiration to aspiring humanity.

By this definition, Asoka was certainly one of the greatest saints of all time. H. G. Wells numbers him among the first six great benefactors of the human race, because by the sheer power of his personality he gave this world its nearest introduction to the Kingdom of Heaven on earth that history has thus far recorded. He left behind such an authentic record of his reign that we are more certain of its extent and character than we are of most of the reigns in Europe throughout the Middle Ages.

Who was king Asoka? He was the third emperor of all India and its first Buddhist king, a contemporary of Ptolemy of Egypt and Antiochus of Syria.

Ascending the throne in 273 B.C., he reigned for forty years. The extent of his empire was greater by far than present India and Pakistan together. Legend has it that Asoka was not the rightful heir to that throne, that he waded through the blood of ninety-nine brothers in order to obtain it for himself. But the higher critics tell us that these stories may be dismissed as the pious fabrications of Buddhist priests who deliberately set out to blacken Asoka's earlier life in order to enhance the transformation that took place after his conversion to the Buddhist faith.

The conversion of Asoka to the Eightfold Path of Buddha was truly one of the most remarkable conversions in the annals of religion, comparable in its suddenness and significance to that of Paul on the road to Damascus.

In the ninth year of his reign, Asoka coveted the territory of a nearby people called the Kalingas and waged a cruel war of conquest against them, killing one hundred thousand, taking another one hundred thousand captive and leaving behind him many thousands maimed and wounded. After it was all over, the brutalities and sufferings which he had so selfishly inflicted upon a helpless people weighted so heavily upon his conscience that when the teachings of Buddha on the sacredness of life were brought to his attention, such was his penitence that he vowed then and there never again to wage war or resort to any form of violence in extending or even preserving the domain of empire.

How different from Xerxes at the Hellespont, David on the plains of Bethlehem, Napoleon after the battle of Austerlitz, or Cortez before the walls of Mexico City! All these conquerors, so we are told, had momentary qualms over the havoc they had wrought, but every one of them went right ahead with his bloody business. Asoka is probably the only instance in all history of a conqueror who truly and sincerely repented of his murderous, butchering activities and renounced the methods of arms and force for the gentler methods of mind and heart — the methods of persuasion and moral example. He was not the first pacifist ruler in history. That distinction belongs to Pharaoh Akhnaton of Egypt. But his reign did not last long enough to constitute a fair test of pacifist policy. The Pharaoh died an early death. Asoka, however, was the first ruler to make pacifism really work and he made it work so successfully, and over such a long period of years that nothing has equalled his reign in moral splendor and social benevolence before or since.

It is no wonder that present-day India is inclined to place confidence in the non-violent peaceful methods of the late Mahatma Gandhi. Its most brilliant era was based upon such a policy.

When king Asoka became converted to Buddhism he did for it what Paul and Constantine did for Christianity. In fact, he did a great deal more. When Constantine gave his preference to Christianity, it was one of the major religions of his empire, whereas Buddhism was merely a local, hopeless sect when king Asoka raised it to a place of world-wide importance. Paul preached to hundreds and thousands. But Asoka literally preached to millions. He did something very

unique in the way of publicizing a religion. He simplified
the teachings of Buddha and incorporated their substance in
fourteen Edicts which he had carved into huge rocks and
monuments all over India, placed in strategic positions and
so carved that these inscriptions could be read at a great
distance by the passer-by.

Seven complete recensions of these huge Rock Edicts are
still in existence today, together with many minor rock and
pillar and cave inscriptions. From these alone, we are able
to reconstruct the history of Asoka's reign and determine
quite accurately the character of the man himself.

In the first place they prove conclusively that king Asoka,
while a Buddhist, was tolerant of other religions. He not
only preached tolerance but practiced it himself. He gave
lavishly to the Jains and Brahmans and built temples for
them, reserving, of course, his major gifts to spread the ethical teaching of his own faith. He permitted freedom of
belief in all religious matters, not because he held that "every
man's religion was right, but that every man's religion was
at some point wrong where some other religion was probably
right and because of this there was danger in suppressing any
man's religion." These are not the words of Asoka, but they
embrace his thought. As far as Asoka was concerned, men
could believe as they pleased so long as they endeavored to
do what was right. The end that he was primarily concerned
with was ethical and spiritual conduct.

From the Twelfth Rock Edict we read, in part, as follows:

. . . there should be a promotion of the essential elements of
Religion in all religions.

This promotion of the essentials of Religion is possible in
many ways.

But its root is restraint of speech; that is to say, there ought
to be no exaltation of one's religion and finding fault with
another's on improper occasion, and there ought to be no de-
preciation of another's religion on this and that occasion.

On the contrary, others' religions should be honored in every way. By so doing one exalts one's own religion and does service to another's religion. By doing otherwise one injures one's own religion and harms another's as well.

For whosoever does honor to his own religion and condemns another's — all through attachment to his own religion — in order to glorify his own religion, is in very truth severely injuring his own religion.

Concourse, fellowship with members of other faiths, is therefore commendable, to the end that they may hear and desire to hear further one another's Dharma (religion).

For this is the desire of the Emperor that all sects and religions shall be well-informed and fruitful of good.

And those who are attached to their respective sects and religions ought to be spoken to as follows:

"Emperor Asoka values neither gifts nor honors so highly as that there should be a promotion of the essential elements of Religion in all religions and mutual appreciation as well." [1]

King Asoka was not only a tolerant king, but he was also a humanitarian king. In fact, "Humane King" was the only title by which others called him and by which he called himself. He preached and practiced the Buddhist doctrine of the sacredness of all life, animal as well as human. Not only did he give up war as a policy of state, but he gave up the slaughter of animals for food and prohibited animal sacrifices in religious rites and ceremonies. He planted shade trees and fruit trees and dug wells every half mile along the highways of India for the comfort of both man and beast. He erected hospitals on a grand scale and cultivated medicinal roots and herbs. He went about his empire in company with the ablest physicians of his court, giving public lectures on health and hygiene, visiting the sick and personally attending to the most needy cases. He paid no attention whatsoever to distinctions of caste, dining with the so-called Untouchables as freely as with priests and princes. In the Indian ocean there was no distinction between the waters of the five great rivers and in the Buddhist brotherhood there was no distinction between the five great castes.

Every year, on the anniversary of his coronation, he granted a general amnesty to all political offenders and as many criminal offenders as his conscience would permit. He is credited by Buddhist tradition with having abolished the death penalty altogether and having placed his entire penology on a reformative instead of a retributive basis. One might imagine that his realm would have been overrun with thieves and cutthroats, but, if we can believe the records, it was not. On the contrary, it was singularly free from crimes against person and property. The state had set a powerful example in the person of the monarch.

Asoka was not only a tolerant humane king, but he was also a democratic king; that is, as democratic as a king is likely to become and still remain a king. He had a well-organized system of government. He had his viceroys, his lieutenants, his commissioners, his secretaries of trade, labor, education, foreign affairs, manufacture and justice, taxes and vital statistics. He publicly announced that these were to serve the people and not to be served. In addition, he proclaimed by means of the Rock Edicts his own readiness to be approached at any hour of the day or night by any man, woman or child who had a grievance to be aired or a supplication to make. He was to be approached whether he was dining, bathing, sleeping, speaking or going on a pilgrimage. No one was to feel the slightest hesitancy in introducing himself because the meanest and humblest citizen in India was the object of his care and sympathy.

Tradition tells us that thousands of people took advantage of the king's magnanimous offer. He was literally swamped with demands for personal ministrations. And yet, in spite of it all he found time to undertake great irrigation projects, to erect thousands of monolithic monuments — some of them four hundred feet high — to build temples and auditoriums, the architectural magnificence of which made Fa Hsien, the

Chinese historian, proclaim them five centuries later to be the work of a supernatural genius.

King Asoka, in spite of a seeming inefficiency, was really superefficient, because his own example of industry inspired the finest talent of his empire to devote itself to the general welfare. His reign resulted, therefore, not only in a religious reformation and widespread prosperity, but in a renaissance of culture and beauty, of architecture and sculpture, song and poetry, and the allied arts.

But he was also a pious king. He preached the law of piety and lived up to it. He denied himself the pleasures of the chase and the drinking bout, and devoted himself to the simple life, to meditation and self-discipline. For a definite period, he joined the order of Buddhist monks and donned their yellow robe. It was possible for him to do this, for Buddhist regulation did not involve a ceremony of lifelong vows. Therefore, the king, for a time, begged his own bread and went on an extended pilgrimage to the various shrines of Buddhism: first to the birthplace of its founder; then to the sacred Bo Tree of Enlightenment; then to the place where Gautama preached his first sermon; and finally to the spot where he was buried. At all of these places he erected monuments with appropriate inscriptions.

His whole life was scrupulously honest, beautifully simple and filled with intellectual as well as moral integrity — as honest as that of Marcus Aurelius, as simple as that of Socrates.

Finally, Asoka was a humanist king, not merely humane. He was not very much concerned about the theology of Buddhism. He was interested in its moral and social teachings. He was anxious that people should adopt the Buddhist way of life, which he proclaimed was the way of truthfulness, sincerity, courage, kindness, gentleness and sobriety. He revised the Buddhist Bible with the plan of eliminating all the

false and superstitious accretions that had gathered about it
since the Eightfold Path had first been promulgated.

Sharing the common Indian faith in reincarnation, he
naturally believed in a future life. Nevertheless he was primarily concerned with this life here. Sharing Buddha's
agnosticism, he refused to affirm or deny the existence of a
Supreme Intelligence. He preached the duty of human self-
reliance, the necessity of every man's working out his own
salvation. In all such matters, he took essentially the attitude
of the religious humanists of today.

Did not this saint have any faults to mar the beauty of his
character? Were there no sins and shortcomings in his life
— no blots and blotches to soil the whiteness of his record?
To be sure, there were, but they were largely due to the
limitations of his day and age.

It is true that he was a polygamist, but so was every Indian
prince and potentate who could afford to be one.

He was a despot — benevolent, prudent, efficient — but still
a despot. Despotism does not appeal to us, however highly
it was regarded in ancient India. But his despotism did bring
forth a reign of righteousness the like of which the world
has never seen before or since.

Asoka was lacking in modesty, inscribing his name all over
his empire and signing himself "the Humane King." But,
after all, he was humane; he was virtuous, sober, industrious
and efficient. He did love mercy. He did dispense justice
and he did go about doing good. His heart was filled with
human compassion, and his hands with human helpfulness.
Repenting fully of the sins of which he was aware, he sincerely made all possible atonement by devoting the larger
part of his life to preaching the truth as he saw it, to overcoming evil with good, and above all by advancing the cause
of peace.

His was the glory which Milton celebrates in the third
book of *Paradise Regained:*

They err who count it glorious to subdue
By conquest far and wide, to over-run
Large countries, and in fields great battle win,
Great cities by assault.
. . . .
But if there be in glory aught of good,
It may by means far different be attained,
Without ambition, war, or violence;
By deeds of peace, by wisdom eminent,
By patience, temperance.

This was truly the glory of the sainted Asoka, a glory which his rock inscriptions have preached through many centuries; a glory which presidents, prime ministers and lesser folk could well afford to take seriously today; a glory which we trust will become inscribed in the hearts of men and nations long before the last edict of Asoka has been effaced from the rocks of India by the ravages of time.

8

Zoroaster and the Struggle Against Evil

> To enjoy the benefits of providence is wisdom; to enable others to enjoy them is virtue. He who is indifferent to the welfare of others does not deserve to be called a man.

> The best way of worshipping God is to allay the distress of the times and to improve the conditions of mankind.

> This is true religion: to cleanse oneself with pure thoughts, words and deeds. He needs no other rosary whose life is strung with beads of loving thought.

> Have the religions of mankind no common ground? Is there not everywhere the same enrapturing beauty, beaming forth from many thousand hidden places?

> Broad indeed is the carpet which the All-loving One has spread, and beautiful the colors he has given it.

> There is but one lamp in his house, in the rays of which, wherever we look, a bright assembly greets us.

> Diversity of worship has divided the human race into countless nations; from all their dogmas we may select one: — Divine Love.

> — ZOROASTRIAN SCRIPTURES

OF ALL THE DISTINGUISHED SAINTS and seers· considered thus far, Western civilization owes more to Zoroaster than to all the others combined, with, of course, the exception of the great Hebrew prophets. He was called Zarathustra by his

own people, the Persians, and known to the Greeks as Zoroas-
tres.

While there are only about one hundred thousand professed followers of Zoroaster left in the world today, the
people of four continents — Europe, Australia, North and
South America — are still largely in the grip of his ideas and
concepts. The hymns and prayers of Christianity bear witness
to the present vitality of his spiritual and theological influence.

The very custom that brings people together for stated
services of worship on Sunday mornings rather than on
Saturday or Monday goes back directly to the mighty impact
of his personality upon the course of history. Yet, mighty
as that impact has been, we scarcely know a single thing
about his life that is authentic. His personality is so hidden
behind a mountain of legend that it is a difficult task to
separate historical facts from religious fiction.

We know nothing about his parentage, nothing about
where or when he was born, except in a most general way.
Indeed some scholars are of the opinion that no such person
as Zoroaster ever lived — just as others tell us that no such
person as Jesus ever lived. But the majority of scholars hold
that the very genius of the Zoroastrian system of thought demands the existence of a unifying personality to account for
its revolutionary form and content.

Applying the same methods of historical criticism to the
Zoroastrian Bible, which have been applied to a study of
our own sacred scriptures, these scholars have come to fairly
reliable conclusions. The Greek historian, Herodotus,
placed the birth of Zoroaster about 5000 years before his
own era. But modern scholars place it somewhere around
the year 660 B.C. There is evidence to believe that he was
still living when the Jews were taken captive into Babylon.

Zoroaster was born in the northwestern part of Persia near
the head waters of the Euphrates River. At an early age

he became disgusted with the corrupt practices of the prevailing religion and was found disputing with the priests
and theologians of his day, just as Jesus disputed with the
rabbis and doctors in the temple at the age of twelve. It was
the ever-present problem of suffering and evil which challenged his imagination, as it has challenged many a sensitive
spirit since. He could not square the presence of evil and
suffering in the world with the idea of a good God, and he
wanted so much to believe in the goodness of God. He set
forth on his own to find some solution for this apparent
contradiction.

For several years he tramped the deserts and mountains
of Persia in search of an answer to his quest, trying, in turn,
the methods of extreme asceticism, monastic communal life
and solitary retreat from all the haunts of civilization. Finally,
after seven years, as he stood before the entrance of a desert
cave, a new insight came to him as suddenly as the light
broke upon Buddha under the Bo Tree. Taking his
shepherd's staff in hand, he went forth to convert his fellow
countrymen to his new found gospel.

The reason why there is suffering, pain, disease, injustice,
pestilence, war, crime in the world, he proclaimed, is very
clear. It is all due to the existence of the Devil. This earth
and the soul of man is the disputed territory of two mighty
opposing forces in the universe. On the one hand we have
Ahura Mazda, the God of life, light and goodness, at the
head of a host of angels and archangels. On the other we
have Angra Mainyu, the God of death, darkness and evil,
at the head of a cohort of demons and devils. Between these
two opposing forces there is a fight to the bitter end. It is
the privilege of man to line up on either side, but if he knows
what is good for himself, he had better side with Ahura
Mazda, because though the battle is going to be a long drawn-
out affair, in the end complete triumph will come to the side
of Ahura Mazda.

Thus the idea of the Devil came into the world's thought for the first time. For up until this time, the pain and suffering of mankind had been due to the punishment of more or less benevolent divinities. Some of them were often vain, fickle, jealous and even spiteful, and had to be placated in order to persuade them to do the right thing. But they were always amenable to persistent prayer, to flattery, praise, or even outright bribery in the form of sacrificial offerings. As a last resort, some could even be tricked and deceived.

But the Devil of Zoroaster was a real implacable devil. He knew his own powers and he could not be deceived or tricked and there was no use in trying to placate him in any way whatsoever. He simply was an unrelenting enemy of the human soul and had to be resisted openly and fought to the bitter end with no thought of ever being able to strike a bargain with him.

Who and where was the Devil? Zoroaster had a specific answer to that. The idea of the Devil may have been suggested by the great physical contrasts which characterized the country of Iran — high mountains, deep valleys; arid deserts, fertile plains; extreme cold in winter, extreme heat in summer; periods of drought and then a long period of torrential rains. So instead of one God responsible for both good and evil, Zoroaster insisted upon two Gods, one responsible for the good — the other for the evil.

He pointed to the Devas, the old gods whom the people had been worshipping. "These are the servants of the evil one," he thundered. "They must be repudiated at once and all their works."

In order to fight against Angra Mainyu, and to fight for Ahura Mazda (who was symbolized by the sun), one must keep Ahura Mazda's fires forever burning on the mountain tops and on all high places and especially on the hearths of every home.

Ahura Mazda is the God of Truth — therefore his worshippers must always tell the truth and keep their contractual obligations. "The liar is a servant of the evil one."

Ahura Mazda is the God of the Harvest. "He who cultivates barley, cultivates virtue. When the wheat appears, the demons hiss. When the grain is ripe, they flee in despair."

Here we see the clash between the nomadic and agrarian ways of life being resolved in favor of the agrarian.

Ahura Mazda is the God of Purity and Righteousness. Those who worship him must not engage in murder, thievery, rape or marital infidelity.

Here is evidence of an emerging urban population endeavoring to maintain some semblance of law and order to protect itself from marauding nomadic tribes.

No matter how great the temptation to side with the evil one, the worshippers of Ahura Mazda must never become discouraged about the final outcome but must strive the harder to live lives of righteousness and purity.

What is all this struggle and striving for? Someday, sooner or later, the conflict between Ahura Mazda and Angra Mainyu will come to an end, and when that day arrives, the mountains and hills will melt and pour down over the earth like molten lava and all the dead will be resurrected from their graves to pass through this boiling stream. To the just and righteous that lava will be as warm milk and they will pass over with laughter and songs of thanksgiving on their lips. But to the wicked and unregenerate, it will be a lake of fire and brimstone and there shall be great weeping and wailing and gnashing of teeth. Forever afterward this earth will be a heavenly paradise wherein there shall be no night or darkness, no sorrow, pain or suffering, no war, no hate, and no death. The glorious kingdom of Ahura Mazda will have come down to earth and man will live forever in eternal peace and joy.

Thus spoke Zoroaster in thunderous voice and fierce sincerity. But for all his eloquence, he could not get anyone to take him seriously. For ten discouraging years he wandered about trying to make converts to his new religion. He was about to give up in despair when he finally succeeded in winning over one of his own cousins. What a real lift of the spirit it is to get one's relatives to believe in one! Zoroaster's one convert gave him enough courage to persevere for two years longer. Then it was that he finally won over to his cause, after a prolonged debate, the mighty king of Persia by the name of Vishtaspa, the grandfather of Darius I, who became the Constantine of this new faith.

The king took drastic measures to stamp out all traces of the old religion, whose gods had become Zoroaster's devils. For thirty-five years these two worked closely together in opposing all the stubborn priests and supporters of the old faith. Tradition claims that Zoroaster was killed by one of these priests while performing a ceremony at the altar fire of Ahura Mazda. He died at the age of seventy-seven.

After his death, strange tales began to gather about his name — tales of how he was really born of a virgin, visited by adoring Magi, saved in infancy from a jealous and powerful foe; tales of how he as a youth confounded the wise men of his day by his precocious knowledge, how he began to preach at the age of thirty, was tempted by the devil in the wilderness, cast out demons, performed miracles by the score and was transported directly to heaven by a host of heavenly angels without having to wait for the final day of judgment. All these tales can be found in the Zend-Avesta, which was written centuries before the Gospels of Matthew and Luke were even thought of.

For two centuries, from 538 B.C. when the Persians conquered Babylon, to 331 B.C., when Alexander the Great conquered Persia, the religion of Zoroaster was the dominant faith of a vast empire that extended from the Mediterranean Sea to the Indian Ocean. After the conquest of Alexander, however, this dualistic religion tended to degenerate into polytheism and undergo many changes. Ahura Mazda came to be called Ormuzd, still later on Mithra, half God and half man, but still a symbol of the sun. Aingra Mainyu came to be called Ahriman and still later Beelzebub. Under the name of Mithraism it succeeded in dominating the larger part of the world of the Eastern Mediterranean Sea and Euphrates Valley, until the time of Constantine, which was well into the fourth century after the birth of Jesus.

In the year 220 A.D., a fresh attempt was made to restore the purity of the original faith of Zoroaster. The Avesta was translated into Greek and Latin and an explanation was added called the Zend; together they are known as the Zend-Avesta. For four hundred years there was considerable activity and ecclesiastical success, but when the Emperor Constantine decided to embrace Christianity, the decline of Zoroaster set in. And later, when Mohammed rose to power by the might of his armies, the doom of this faith was finally sealed. Its adherents were reduced to a feeble remnant.

Today there are only about one hundred thousand left, ninety thousand Parsees in India, as they are called — and in Persia, the land of its origin, only ten thousand are still loyal to the faith. Nevertheless, the influence of Zoroaster is as dominant today as it ever has been, yes, even more so. Both Catholic and Protestant Christianity are still in the mighty grip of his theological thought; and also Orthodox Judaism, though to a lesser degree.

The prevailing theology in Europe and America today is founded upon a dualistic conception of the universe. There are two great Powers in life, a Power making for righteousness and a Power making for evil. On the one hand we have a good God and on the other his Satanic Majesty, the Devil.

Where did we get the idea of the Devil? We got it from the Jews and the Jews got it from the Persians when they were taken captive, into Babylon. Before that time, the religion of Israel had been without a Satan. There is no mention in the Jewish scriptures of Satan until after the Babylonian Exile. Until that time, Jehovah was the author of both good and evil, the evil that came to men was God's punishment for sin. But, after the Babylonian Exile, a great change took place in Jewish theology. All the evils which the priests could not explain as punishment for sin, were laid at the door of the Devil and his cohorts.

The word Devil is Persian in origin. The old gods whom Zoroaster overthrew were called Devas. They became the devils of his new religion. Both the good and the bad meanings are still preserved for us in the two words, "divinity" and "deviltry."

Whenever we use the expression, "The good fight of faith" we are thinking after the manner of Zoroaster, for we cannot escape the idea that there is something in the universe against which we must struggle. The concept of life as a battle royal, a colossal moral crusade, the outcome of which depends on man's courage and effort, is a far more ennobling concept than that of man as a helpless worm in the dust or a cog in a machine or the plaything of fate.

The second idea which we can lay at the door of Zoroaster is the idea of Hell, an idea which still dominates the religious thinking of a large part of the Western world. This too we can trace back to its origin in the Persian prophet. The Sheol of pre-exilic Israel was like the Hades of the Greek and Roman world, a shadowy realm of disembodied spirits who lived an empty existence, empty of pain and sorrow as well as of pleasure and joy.

Hell as a place of torment — a lake burning with fire and brimstone, where there is weeping and wailing and gnashing of teeth — began with Zoroaster. Those who believe in this kind of after-life are under the spell of an ancient Persian's imagination. When Dante wrote his *Divine Comedy* and described in vivid detail the various levels of Hell, he was merely making a blueprint of an architectural plan suggested by a master architect, who had lived centuries before him.

A third idea that can be traced to Zoroaster is the doctrine of the resurrection of the body.

Liberals and modernists do not accept the theory today. But in Catholic and orthodox Protestant circles, belief in the resurrection of the body is still an important article of faith.

Whence does it come? Surely not from the Greeks or Egyptians for they believed only in the resurrection of the soul of man. Nor from the ancient Hebrews before the Babylonian Exile, for they did not believe in resurrection. Modern scholars trace it directly to the influence of Zoroaster, coming into Judaism by way of the prophet Ezekiel at the time of the Exile, and into Christianity by way of Judaism and the mystical cult of Mithra which was the big rival of early Christianity.

The angel Gabriel sounding his trumpet on the final day of judgment in order to arouse the dead from their graves was preached in Persia long before either the Jewish Pharisees or the early Christians appeared upon the scene.

In the fourth place, our observance of Sunday as a day of worship, together with our celebration of Christmas and Easter, go back ultimately to the same source. It is very clear now that Christianity took these institutions over bodily from the mystery cult of Mithraism, which in turn had inherited them from the older religion of Zoroaster. Ahura Mazda and Mithra were both symbolized by the sun. Christmas and Easter marked important turning points in the yearly cycle of the sun. The Magi were priests of Ahura Mazda, the God of light and life. We still use the word "magic" to describe the wonders of the Magi and the word Mazda to name an electric light. The Magi conducted their regular services of worship on Sunday. When the early Christians went forth into the Gentile world, they found it more convenient to hold their meetings on this day rather than on the Jewish Sabbath and rationalized it by calling it the "Lord's Day." When Jesus used the word "paradise," he was using not only a Persian concept but also the Persian word for it.

Thus, it is easy to see, the major portion of orthodox Christian theology and tradition has its origin in Zoroaster. Some of this inheritance religious liberals regard as pure speculation and even superstition.

For example, while we cannot disprove the existence of His Satanic Majesty, we are, shall we say, very much inclined to disbelieve it. We surely fear no Hell of fire and brimstone in the hereafter. We dismiss the idea of a bodily resurrection as a most unlikely prospect. We regard the angel Gabriel and his trumpet a figment of the imagination.

We frankly acknowledge that our Christmas and Easter festivals have their origin in solar myths, but see no point in changing these festivals to other dates and even much good in observing ancient customs by filling them with fresh and meaningful content.

We accept the custom of worshipping on Sunday as a matter of convenience but do not regard it as more sacred than the rest of the days of the week; or, may we add, the rest of the days of the week as less sacred than Sunday.

We stand in no dread of a final day of judgment and look for no sudden intervention from the skies to usher in a millennial kingdom on earth.

With Zoroaster's theology, we are either at loggerheads or mildly indifferent; with Zoroaster's ethics, however, we are in perfect and hearty agreement.

When Zoroaster states that life is a fight against evil, we approve of his insight. His practical moral teaching might be paraphrased in these words: Haughty thoughts and thirst for gold are sins; angry words and scornful looks are sins; reply to thine enemy with gentleness and love; avoid everything calculated to injure others; treat old age with reverence and sympathy; be very careful to speak the truth in all things; take not that which belongs to another.

His golden rule, "That nature alone is good which shall not do unto another whatever is not good unto its own self,"[1] we heartily endorse. He further declares in the *Avesta* that man's duty is threefold: "To make him who is an enemy a friend, to make him who is wicked righteous; and to make him who is ignorant learned."[2] We say these are surely worthy ideals.

With this ethical religion we can readily agree. For it has produced among the Parsees of India and Persia as fine a type of character as can be found anywhere upon the face of this earth — men who live beautiful lives of nobleness and charity, of peacefulness and truth, such as the late Jeejeebhoy of Bombay, a distinguished philanthropist, and the lyrical poet Saadi of Persia.

"As binding as the word of a Parsee" has become a proverb.

The Greek historian, Herodotus, noted that it was the custom of the followers of this faith "to ascend to the highest peaks of the mountains, and offer sacrifice to Zeus. . . . It is not permitted to him who sacrificeth to ask for good things for his own private use; but he maketh petition for good to befall the whole Persian people."[3]

Because of the high ethical content of this religion, the world can ill afford to neglect its altar fires. We must see to it that whatever is inspiring in its sacred scriptures is added to our Bible and claim its prophet as one of our very own. We must join his crusade against the powers and principalities of darkness in this world. For we too would fight the good fight of faith.

9

The Hebrew Prophets and the Heart of Religion

> Wherewith shall I come before the Lord, and bow
> myself before the high God? shall I come before him
> with burnt-offerings, with calves of a year old?
>
> Will the Lord be pleased with thousands of rams,
> or with ten thousands of rivers of oil? shall I give my
> first born for my transgression, the fruit of my body
> for the sin of my soul?
>
> He hath shewed thee, O man, what is good; and
> what doth the Lord require of thee, but to do justly,
> and to love mercy, and to walk humbly with thy God?
>
> — MICAH

WHAT DOES IT MEAN TO BE RELIGIOUS?

Many definitions of religion have been given, some more
pertinent than others. The late George Gordon of the Old
South Church in Boston once defined religion as "the life
of God in the soul of man." The late Bishop Rainsford of
the Episcopal Church once defined it as "the giving of the
best that one has to the highest that one knows." Both of
these definitions are fairly comprehensive.

James, the author of the Epistle, declared, "Pure religion
and undefiled before our God and Father is this, to visit the
fatherless and widows in their affliction, and to keep himself
unspotted from the world." Here is a definition specific in
its ethical implications but not quite as comprehensive as
the first two.

Jesus himself never used the word religion, but this, of course, is what he meant when he attempted to sum up the Law and the Prophets: ". . . thou shalt love the Lord thy God with all thy heart, and with all thy soul, and with all thy mind, and with all thy strength. The second is this. Thou shalt love thy neighbor as thyself. There is none other commandment greater than these." And there is, in truth, no other commandment greater than these.

However, there is a much older summation of religion which tells us much more specifically what love to God and one's neighbor really involves. It can be found inscribed on many a public building in this and other countries. It is the well-known text from the prophecy of Micah. "What doth the Lord require of thee, but to do justly, and to love mercy, and to walk humbly with thy God?"

Here we have a definition of religion that is at once simple, comprehensive, ethical and intelligible. It has never been surpassed and is not likely to be. This sentence which has gone around the world first came from the lips of a plain simple farmer who lived near Jerusalem in the eighth century B.C. He probably had no formal education but apparently was well read in the history of his nation's past, and was thoroughly acquainted with what was going on in Jerusalem and in the surrounding cities and nations. He must have been possessed of a gifted personality with a natural talent for eloquent speech, for when he went up to the city of Jerusalem, large crowds gathered to hear what he had to say and were held spellbound by what they heard.

Micah, the layman, with a directness and sureness remarkable for that or any other age, succeeded in penetrating to the very heart of religion. Where did this self-educated man get his ideas? Whence came his insight and inspiration? For no genius, however original, is wholly original. We know that three of the greatest prophets ever produced by the Hebrew people had just preceded Micah. All had been living when he was born — Amos, Hosea and Isaiah. Each one of these had just made a distinctive contribution to an understanding of vital religion. Amos and Hosea had performed their labors in the Northern Kingdom, the doom of whose capital city, Samaria, both had predicted with uncanny accuracy. Isaiah, an older contemporary of Micah, had performed his chief labors in the Southern Kingdom whose capital city, Jerusalem, for some strange reason not yet fully understood, had for the time being escaped destruction at the hands of the Assyrian hordes who had originally intended to make a clean sweep of both cities.

In this crucial period of great national peril and religious bewilderment, one of the most crucial in the history of the Hebrew people, four men stood out from the rest of their contemporaries for their capacity to discern the signs of the times and to predict accurately the future trend of events. Amos, Hosea and Isaiah each emphasized an important aspect in a trinity of spiritual values — justice, mercy and humility — which the fourth and younger prophet, Micah, brought together into one comprehensive statement, "What doth the Lord require of thee, but to do justly, and to love mercy, and to walk humbly with thy God?"

Whence came Micah's concept of justice? Without doubt from the prophet Amos, both directly and indirectly. Amos, who disclaimed any connection with the profession of prophecy, was a shepherd from the rugged hill country south of Jerusalem. He saw how cities to the east, west, north and south, were going down in ruin, one after another, before the might of the Assyrian aggression — cities whose walls were once thought to be impregnable against any foe. Amos discerned with statesmanlike ability that these cities were falling, not primarily because of the power of the Assyrian armies, but rather because they had all been weakened first from within by widespread disunion and corruption. He saw how every man was out seeking his own interest in direct defiance of the general welfare. The rulers were incompetent and unscrupulous and shamelessly negligent of even the most elementary rights and needs of their people. Luxury and bribery prevailed in high places. Religion was a respectable but superstitious rite, entirely devoid of ethical content. The priests of religion were complacent before the most glaring evils, wholly unaware of the depths of degradation into which they had allowed their nation to sink. They could not see that the very injustice which they were permitting to go on unchallenged was eating at the vitals of the body politic and eventually would so weaken the nation as to make it an easy prey for any determined foe. But Amos saw the danger clearly, and tried to warn in time the Northern Kingdom which was directly in the path of the Assyrian aggression. He boldly told the people of Samaria that they could no longer tolerate injustice in their midst and expect to survive.

Hear this, O ye that swallow up the needy,
And make the poor of the land to fail,
Saying, When will the new moon be gone, that we may sell corn?
And the sabbath, that we may set forth wheat?
Ye that make the measure small, and the shekel great,
That falsify the balance by deceit,
That buy the poor for silver,
And the needy for a pair of sandals;
Hear ye the word of the Lord:
I hate, I despise your feast days,
And I delight not in your solemn assemblies.
Though ye offer me burnt offerings,
I will not accept them;
Neither will I regard the peace offerings of your fat beasts.
Take away from me the noise of thy songs!
For I will not hear the melody of thy viols.
But let justice roll down as waters,
And righteousness as an overflowing stream.
Hate the evil, and love the good,
And establish justice in the gate:
Then shall the Lord God of hosts
Be gracious unto you and hear you.

When Amos made this speech it was a startling pronounce-
ment. He identified true worship with private and public
righteousness. Religious people had not been in the habit
of thinking in such terms. The thought came to them like a
bolt from a blue sky. They could scarcely believe their ears.
But the declaration of Amos was a great step forward in the
development of religious thinking, a bold insight which has
lost none of its shocking force, because apparently there are
would-be religious people even today who cannot quite grasp
the truth that righteousness, private and public, is the first
and most fundamental requirement of ethical religion, and
no one is exempt therefrom, from the least to the greatest in
the nation. Internal justice is the front line of defense for
any nation.

To do justly, however, is not enough. To love mercy is
equally required of man.

Mercy is a bold concept. To many it has the connotation
of weakness, or weak-mindedness, or even appeasement. Few
people have fully grasped the idea that only the strong can
be merciful. Mercy goes beyond justice. It is more than fair.
It is generous and forgiving. As God loves mercy, so should
man love mercy.

Whence came Micah's emphasis on mercy as one of a trinity
of religious requirements? From his older contemporary,
Hosea, without doubt. Not that Hosea originated the idea,
for it had long existed in the background of Hebrew thought,
but the great contribution of Hosea was that he brought it
out into the foreground. Amos proclaimed a God of stern
justice. But Hosea went further. He proclaimed a God of
justice *and* mercy. At the heart of the universe, he declared,
presides the Will of compassionate and redemptive love, who
is greatly pained whenever the children of men have to suffer
for their sins, but is ever eager to hold out the hope of forgiveness and another chance.

This insight of the prophet came from a sad and painful

experience in his own personal life.[1] Hosea loved a beautiful woman by the name of Gomer, to whom he was married. Three times this wife proved unfaithful to her marriage vows, and gave birth to a child of whom Hosea was not the father. Hebrew justice entitled Hosea to an immediate divorce and called for the stoning to death of the unfaithful wife and the holding up to public scorn of her illegitimate children. But Hosea could not find it in his heart to take advantage of the law of justice and thus be responsible for such direful retribution. On each occasion he was able to rise above the pain in his own heart and take his wife back into his affection, and assume the support of her innocent offspring. He made the amazing discovery that it is more important to love than to be loved, to suffer bravely an unmerited sorrow than to seek temporary compensation in adding to the sorrows of others. There is no doubt that Gomer crushed the heart of Hosea, but the prophet's love for her was so great and compelling that he was able to transcend the bitterness of his own disappointment and reach an exalted understanding of the nature of all life.

The capacity to forgive which he found within his own soul he attributed to the love of God. The heart of the Eternal One, he declared, is long-suffering and most wonderfully kind. Just as he, Hosea, had learned to look with compassion on his wayward wife, so God looks upon the infidelity of his people. It is not the will of Heaven that Ephraim (the Northern Kingdom) and Judah (the Southern Kingdom) should be cast away forever and destroyed.

What can I do with thee? O Ephraim?
What can I do with thee? O Judah!
Since your love is like the morning cloud
And like the dew goes early away.
Therefore I have hewn them by the prophets.
. . . .
And my judgment is like the light that goes forth.

For it is love that I have desired and not sacrifice,
And the knowledge of God rather than burnt-offerings.

. . . .

Lo! Ephraim has become like a silly dove, without understanding.
They cry to Egypt, they go to Assyria.

. . . .

How can I give thee up, O Ephraim?
How can I let thee go, O Israel?
My heart is turned within me;
My compassions are kindled together.

. . . .

A spirit of harlotry has led them astray,
And they have played the harlot away from their God.

. . . .

But behold, I will heal their backsliding.
I will love them freely,
For mine anger is turned away from them.

Here we have a depiction of Deity that has never been surpassed in eloquence and tenderness. And let us not forget when it was uttered — eight centuries before Jesus, four centuries before Mo Ti, the Chinese sage, three centuries before the birth of the Buddha, all of whom reached essentially the same great insight — that the reality behind our life is not only just but also full of compassion and mercy.

"What doth the Lord require of thee but to do justly, and to love mercy, *and* to walk humbly with thy God?" What does Micah mean by "walking humbly with God"? Why is humility such a cardinal religious virtue? Whence came the concept? For answer we must refer once again to one of the prophets who immediately preceded Micah, for Micah was here merely summing up in one phrase the major contribution which Isaiah had just made to the development of Hebrew thinking.

Let us consider the situation as it then existed. Isaiah was a citizen of the Southern Kingdom whose capital was Jerusalem. Isaiah, unlike Amos and Hosea, was a man of birth and position, influential in court circles, a statesman who strove to secure justice at home, to counsel wisdom in foreign relationships, and to make true religion a vital factor in both the individual and national life of the people.

One day, early in his career, Isaiah had a strange mystical experience in the temple at Jerusalem. Call it hallucination, supersensory perception, a dream, or what you will — but in that temple, empty at the time, he saw a light and heard a voice like nothing he had ever seen or heard before; and from that time forth, Isaiah was convinced of the reality of a Divine Presence in his life whom he could never doubt, and whom he was inspired to call "The Lord of Hosts, the Holy One of Israel."

But not long after this experience, came the destruction of Samaria at the hands of the Assyrians and the captivity of the ten northern tribes. This confronted Isaiah and the people of Jerusalem with an urgent religious problem. If the Holy One of Israel is indeed the Lord of Hosts, why was the city of Samaria allowed to be destroyed? For these ten northern tribes worshipped at the shrines of the same faith as the Southern Kingdom. Was the God of Assyria more powerful than the God of Israel? What was the use of worshipping a Deity who cannot protect his own domain? A weak and helpless God is worse than no God at all. Thus argued the man on the street. The people of Palestine, after the fall of Samaria, were precisely in the same religious predicament as the people of Japan were after the crushing defeat of their military forces. Having identified the Deity with the Emperor, and the Emperor having been proved a broken reed and forced to renounce all claims to deity, Shintoism, the religion of Japan, is at the present time in a dire state of confusion. It is being obliged to make some very drastic changes in order to hold the loyalty of its former adherents. "The American God must be more powerful than the Japanese God," the common people are thinking, if not actually saying in so many words.

In the days of Isaiah religion was up against precisely the same problem. People were openly denying the existence of their nation's deity, and rapidly discarding all their former moral scruples. Before the fall of Samaria, Jerusalem, like all cities in that period, had had its full share of corruption and lawlessness, but after the fall of Samaria that lawlessness turned into a veritable riot of license and self-indulgence. Losing their faith in Deity, the people lost their heads. "Where there is no vision, the people cast off restraint."

But, Isaiah stepped into the breach and gave the people a vision once more. He gave them a vision of a God transcending in majesty, power, and holiness anything they had worshipped before. He could not doubt the reality of his early experience with the Divine Presence. No! There is nothing wrong with Israel's God, he shouted. Jehovah is not weak and helpless but strong and mighty. He is not only the God of Israel and Judah but of Assyria and all the nations of the earth as well. If Israel has suffered severely at the hands of Assyria, it is because Assyria has been used by the Deity merely as an instrument to punish Israel for her awful wickedness and corruption.

"Ho! Assyria, the rod of mine anger and the staff of mine indignation." This was Isaiah's answer to the religious confusion of his day. The trouble that has befallen the Northern Kingdom has come to pass not because there is something wrong with the Eternal One but because there was something wrong with Israel. And the same fate awaits the unrighteous people of Judah. Unless they humble themselves before the majesty of the Holy One of Israel and do so at once, the same fate will be meted out to them.

> Woe unto them that call evil good, and good evil;
> That put darkness for light, and light for darkness;
> That put bitter for sweet, and sweet for bitter!
> Woe unto them that are wise in their own eyes,
> And prudent in their own sight!

. . . .

Behold, the haughtiness of man shall be bowed down,
And the lofty looks of man shall be brought low,
And the Lord alone shall be exalted.

. . . .

Lo, your hands are full of blood!
Wash you, make you clean!
Put away the evil of your doings from before mine eyes;
Cease to do evil, learn to do well;
Seek justice, relieve the oppressed;
Judge the fatherless, plead for the widow.

. . . .

For thus saith the Lord of Hosts,
The Holy One of Israel:
"In returning and rest shall ye be saved,
In quietness and confidence shall be your strength."

God, thundered the prophet, is not impotent but almighty. He is never defeated but always triumphant. For He is the power behind all nations. His righteous will must be served because He, Himself, is Holy and Righteous and All-Prevailing.

Arrogance, pride, conceit keep both men and nations from discovering what that will is. Therefore, both men and nations must repent of their arrogance which always brings on waywardness and disaster, and seek to serve in sincere humility the larger and wider purposes of the God who is above all nations.

This was indeed a stroke of religious genius that eventually exerted a profound influence upon the people of Judah. It was a turning point in their history. If Isaiah and the other great Hebrew prophets had not lived, the Hebrew faith would have died out long ago like many a neighboring tribal cult. But these prophets gave it something indestructible to hold it together; they gave it the inspiring vision of justice, mercy, and humility. This trinity of values which Micah gathered together into one eloquent statement constitutes the heart of real religion. It is the way of salvation. Though never fully achieved by the Jewish people at any time, these values have enabled them to survive the disasters of many centuries because never at any time have they quite lost sight of their great vision.

If there is any lesson to be learned from history, it is that nations are seldom if ever destroyed from without until they have first destroyed themselves from within. They destroy themselves from within by indulging in injustice, in hatred, and in arrogance. If our nation would survive, it must keep ever before it the vision of Micah's trinity of ideals. For justice makes for internal unity and strength. Mercy makes for reconciliation among conflicting interests and for the reformation of the people. Humility is the prime prerequisite for an understanding of what is real and what is illusion.

If this nation is not to go down like so many others before it, our people must strive for the general welfare, we must cultivate generous and magnanimous attitudes toward all kinds and conditions of men, transcending the barriers of race, class, creed, and clime. We must ever seek to distinguish between reality and the distortions which come from arrogance and self-righteousness, and the pride that goeth before a fall. Arrogance says, "I know all the answers. No one can tell me what I should do. I shall do as I please. There is none to stop me. I shall be a law unto myself."

Humility says, "The moral law is the will of God. That will is reality and cannot be ignored without disastrous consequences. Therefore I shall strive to know that will. I shall do, not what I please but what I ought. I shall seek to serve the larger and wider purpose."

"What doth the Lord require of thee, but to do justly, and to love mercy, and to walk humbly with thy God?" This is indeed the heart of vital religion. This is the way of individual salvation. This is the way of national survival.

IO

Socrates and the Search for Truth

> Beloved Pan, and all ye other gods who haunt this
> place, give me beauty in the inward soul; and may
> the outward and inward man be at one. May I reckon
> the wise to be the wealthy, and may I have such a
> quantity of gold as a temperate man and he only can
> bear and carry.
>
> — SOCRATES

FOUR HUNDRED AND SEVENTY YEARS before Jesus preached his
first sermon in the Jewish synagogue at Nazareth, there
walked the streets of another and more ancient city, a strange
and slovenly figure — unkempt, grotesque, flat-nosed, thick-
lipped, barefooted, bareheaded, and bald. He was one of
the homeliest specimens of humanity who ever lived and yet
withal a merry twinkle in his eye and a whimsical smile on
his face. Because this man once walked the city streets of
Athens, this earth is a different place in which to live.

From the day of his birth the world should date its calendar
of philosophy, science, and education. For many of the principles that guide modern science, many of the fundamental
ideas behind our present form of government, some of the
educational methods used at the present hour in our schools
and colleges, and several of the religious values cherished
today — especially in liberal circles — can be traced back
directly and indirectly to the powerful influence of the
homely figure who walked the streets of Athens some twenty-
four centuries ago.

All informed citizens ought to be as familiar with the life of Socrates as they are with the life of Jesus. To both we owe an enormous debt of gratitude. Here are some of the numerous tributes that have been paid by philosophers and historians to the greatness of Socrates.

"I thank God," wrote Plato, "that I was born a Greek and not a barbarian, a freeman and not a slave, a man and not a woman. But above all I thank God that I was born in the age of Socrates."

"The time will come," says Frederick Nietzsche, "when men will turn to the teachings of Socrates as they now turn to the teachings of the Bible."

"Socrates," declares a famous English philosopher, "was the originating genius of common sense, the great teacher of moral and intellectual veracity, one of the profoundest influences in our Anglo-Saxon civilization."

Still another English philosopher rates him as "one of the five great intellects of all time, the least fanatical, the most sane of all the teachers of mankind."

Socrates was born in Athens twenty years after the Battle of Marathon. It was 470 B.C. or thereabouts. It may have been one year earlier or one year later, no one knows exactly. For this and most of the information regarding Socrates we are indebted to Plato, the poet-philosopher, and Xenophon, the soldier-historian, both of them pupils of the great Athenian.

Socrates like Jesus did not leave behind any writings of his own, or if he did, they have not come down to us. There are many myths and legends about this man, of course, but they have been long since discarded by the historians. There are absolutely no authentic references to him by any writer outside of Greece. Take away Plato and Xenophon and the world would know next to nothing concerning Socrates.

Those who accept the historicity of the Greek philosopher and doubt the historicity of the Jewish carpenter should bear this fact in mind when they complain about the scarcity of foreign references to Jesus. It is just as plausible to argue that the one is a creation of Xenophon and Plato as that the other is a creation of Matthew, Mark, Luke and John. Most scholars today accept the historicity of both.

Socrates was born a free Athenian citizen. His father was a tombstone cutter by occupation and a sculptor of fair ability. Socrates was early destined to follow in the footsteps of his father and become a worker in granite and marble. But somehow he did not take very kindly to the routine of tombstone cutting or the art of sculpture. Granite and marble were not hard enough substances for him to waste his time upon. He decided to do his carving on the minds of his fellow men, than which there is nothing harder or more challenging.

Accordingly he gave up sculpture and took up philosophy, with the result that the world is perhaps poorer in tombstones and statues but surely richer in ideas and principles.

An oracle told him that he was the wisest man in Athens. How could this be? How could he be the wisest man in Athens when he knew that he knew very little indeed, unless this awareness of his own ignorance made him far superior to the so-called wise men who also knew very little but did not know even that much.

Intellectual humility is the beginning of wisdom. This is the great discovery which he made. It is impossible to learn if one already thinks one knows it all. From this time forth Socrates took upon himself the task of disclosing the ignorance of everyone he met who claimed to know more than he actually did. He therefore engaged in conversation with all sorts and conditions of men in the market place, on the city streets, in the temple courts, and in the public forum. He spent so much time away from home that one might wonder whether he had a home.

Yes, he had a home but he was fortunately unhappily

married. For a man can be fortunately married without being happily married. Xantippe, the wife of Socrates, made
life so miserable for her husband at home that he found it
more desirable to spend much of his time away from it.
Whenever he came home, she met him at the door with a
withering look and a torrent of words. She scolded him for
being the laughing-stock of the neighborhood.

Perhaps no woman could have made home life attractive
for a man like Socrates. Perhaps if Xantippe had been a
tenderhearted woman there would have been a different
story to tell — most likely no story at all. Apparently the
interests of society are not always served by a happy marriage.
The world owes a great debt of gratitude to some of its
sharp tongued women who have driven their husbands to
find compensation in signal service to the rest of the world.

How he managed to earn his livelihood we do not know,
probably by small sporadic offerings from his pupils. We
do know that he was conscientious about paying his bills. He
lived very simply — on olives, grapes and wine. He went
barefooted and bareheaded and wore the same garments winter and summer. He did this not because he believed there was
any virtue in poverty, but in order to be free for the greater
delights of life. His greatest delight was to learn something
new by asking people questions, and what a multitude of
questions he asked — about war and politics, marriage and
divorce, love and friendship, religion and art, poetry and
science, education and ethics, physics and economics, medicine and cosmetics.

No subject which had any relation to human welfare
escaped his attention. The range of his intellectual interests
was phenomenal. He not only asked questions about these
subjects but he had something to say about every one of them.

He insisted particularly upon precise definitions. He con-
tended that much of the misunderstanding between people
was due to the careless use of words. They thought they

differed in ideas when they were merely differing in vocabulary. People often used the same word with altogether different meanings in the background of their minds, without ever realizing it.

Socrates had a merry time in exposing the fuzzy thinking of his contemporaries in this respect. What a merry time he would have were he living today and were he allowed to circulate in the halls of Congress and the United Nations to ask impertinent questions as to what men meant when they used the words Democracy, Communism, Fascism, Americanism, and Atheism. When today's most hated label of "Communist" can be attached to respectable Republicans, Democrats and Socialists, as well as self-confessed Communists, it is time a Socrates appeared to untangle our confusion.

The proper study of mankind, he declared, is "man." He was not interested at all in nature but profoundly interested in human nature. Fields and trees and stones could not teach him anything which he could not learn from the life of these city streets. Accordingly, he never left those city streets except when he was called upon to become a soldier and fight for his country, a task which he executed with conspicuous bravery and ability.

While Socrates was in the camp of the Athenian army there happened to him the strangest and most important experience in his life. One day this soldier of more than ordinary physical strength found his feet rooted to the ground. He could not move them in any direction, no matter how hard he struggled. Thus pinned to the earth, he remained for twenty-four hours in a trance. His body was reduced to impotence and his spirit caught up into the heavenly regions. Like Paul on the road to Damascus, he saw a great light and heard a strange voice. Like Joan of Arc, that light and that voice continued to abide with him throughout the remainder of his life.

From that day forth he was a different man. He never went

against the warning of his friendly angel or daimon as he called it. Whether the voice he heard was the voice of conscience, the echo of his own common sense, the hallucination of a sensitive nervous system, or something entirely different, we do not know. We only know that Socrates himself was convinced of an objective spiritual reality exterior to himself and strangely wise and ethical in its warnings. He claimed it went with him wherever he went, it stopped wherever he stopped, it was an ever-present companion. It got him into all kinds of difficulties, but it conferred upon him the poise and courage and confidence of divinity itself.

Let us consider but two of several outstanding instances.

After the naval disaster of Arginusae in 406 B.C., eight Athenian commanders were brought to trial for neglecting to recover all the bodies of the slain and wounded. They had done their best under the circumstances but their best was not good enough. The Athenian populace were wild with frenzy and revenge. They demanded the death penalty for every one of the eight commanders. It so happened that it fell to the lot of Socrates to preside over the Athenian Assembly the day this question came up for decision. The guardian angel of Socrates warned him that it was morally wrong even to put the matter to a vote. At first his colleagues agreed with him, but eventually they all gave in to the popular clamor. Socrates alone stood out and resisted to the last and almost lost his own life for his pains. The following day, the Athenians had their way, Socrates being no longer president of the Assembly. History can show few examples of such brave defiance of popular frenzy.

There is Gamaliel, the learned doctor of law, who pleaded for the lives of Peter and John before the Jewish Sanhedrin. There is Thomas Paine who defied the bloodthirsty wrath of the French Parliament to vote against the execution of the king. There is Wendell Phillips who faced the fury of a

Boston mob to defend the rights of William Lloyd Garrison who had just been dragged through the city streets. Would that this sobering presence of Socrates were with us today to guide America in this critical juncture of momentous decisions.

For America stands in real peril today both from without and from within our country. The peril from without is obvious. The peril from within is not so obvious because it is twofold. There is the peril that comes from those who would openly subvert our government if they could. But there is also the peril that comes from those who would subvert our government in order to get at subversives. America faces a grave danger from its own present fears. A wave of hysteria has come over our people and especially our Congress. In an attempt to save the American way of life, measures are now being taken, from the most patriotic of motives, that may jeopardize it.

Once the spirit of thought and speech control takes possession of a country, there is no telling when or where it will strike, or whom. When Robespierre gave his sanction to the repressive measures of the French Revolution in the name of liberty, little did he dream that he himself would be destroyed by the very terror he had helped to unleash. Once the demon of repression is allowed to get under way, it is no respecter of persons and has no patience with reason, logic or evidence. All it needs to wreak vengeance on its victims is fear and suspicion.

Let us hear Socrates as he attempted to show his fellow-citizens of Athens wherein they were subverting their own government under conditions of fear and hysteria.

In 400 B.C. a group of superpatriots seized the seats of power in Athens. They began to persecute all who presumed to challenge their pretensions. Socrates, the most loyal of Athenians, was officially charged with subversion, with denying the gods and corrupting the youth of the city. His guardian angel, instead of counselling him to flee for his own life, marched him right up to the trial assembly as though it were the greatest of good fortunes. In a masterful and eloquent plea which Socrates made without preparation, he defended himself against his accusers.

Instead of denying the gods, he claimed that no one had obeyed them with greater fidelity than he, for his daimon or guardian angel, whose voice he had followed, is the very messenger of the gods. Instead of corrupting the youth of Athens, he marshalled evidence to show that he had inspired his pupils to be nobler and wiser citizens and a credit to the city.

All his evidence and eloquence were in vain, however. The populace had prejudged his case and clamored for his life. A vote was taken and the verdict was 281 to 220 against him. The death penalty was pronounced.

He was given an opportunity to make a farewell address in which he rose to sublime heights. He said in part:

And now, O men who have condemned me, I would fain prophesy to you; for I am about to die, and in the hour of death men are gifted with prophetic power. And I prophesy to you who are my murderers, that immediately after my departure punishment far heavier than you have inflicted on me will surely await you. Me you have killed because you wanted to escape the accuser, and not to give an account of your lives. But that will not be as you suppose; far otherwise. For I say that there will be more accusers of you than there are now; accusers whom hitherto I have restrained; and as they are younger they will be more inconsiderate with you, and you will be more offended at them. If you think that by killing men you can prevent some one from censuring your evil lives, you are mistaken; that is not a way of escape which is either possible or honourable; the easiest and the noblest way is not to be disabling others, but to be improving yourselves. This is the prophecy which I utter before my departure to the judges who have condemned me. . . . I am not angry with my condemners, or with my accusers; they have done me no harm, although they did not mean to do me any good; and for this I may gently blame them. . . .

The hour of departure has arrived, and we go our ways — I to die, and you to live. Which is better God only knows.[1]

Ordinarily, the death penalty would have been carried out the following day. But it so happened that it was the month of a religious festival when a special deputation sailed to the island of Delos. As long as the ship was away on its sacred mission, no death penalty could be carried out in Athens.

On the day before it returned, some of the condemned man's friends came to him with money and plans for him to escape from prison and flee to another country. The details had been carefully worked out and we may presume they would have insured his escape. But Socrates, with true nobility of character, refused to be a party to the scheme. Such was his reverence for the city of his birth, he was resolved not to disobey its laws even though it had done him a grave injustice. To this point of view his friends were finally but reluctantly won.

The day and the hour of his death drew near. He bathed himself in preparation for the great adventure. He bade his wife and sons a fond farewell and gave them final instructions. He called for the cup of hemlock to be prepared and brought in to him at once. His friends demurred and tried to delay the ordeal until late in the evening, but Socrates was anxious to get on with it and had his way.

The warden with trembling hands brought the cup of poison and gave him the proper instructions. Socrates took the cup without any trembling of his hands or change of color in his countenance. With a steady glance at his friends, he lifted the cup to his lips and then drank slowly, calmly, even cheerfully.

When his friends saw the empty vessel, they broke down and began to weep, first one and then another, until they were all weeping, all except Socrates, who remained as calm and composed as ever. Indeed he rebuked his friends for their lack of self-control.

"What is this strange outcry? he said. I sent away the women mainly in order that they might not offend in this way, for I have been told that a man should die in peace. Be quiet then, and have patience."[2]

At the sound of his voice, their sobbing ceased, for they were naturally ashamed of their weakness.

While waiting for the poison to perform its deadly task, Socrates continued to engage his friends in conversation. His last words had reference to the Athenian custom of giving a thank-offering to the deity of medicine, which was done on recovering from a long illness — Socrates regarding death as a possible deliverance from the illness of life itself.

"Crito, I owe a cock to Asclepius; will you remember to pay the debt? The debt shall be paid, said Crito; is there anything else? There was no answer to this question; but in a minute or two a movement was heard, and the attendants uncovered him; his eyes were set, and Crito closed his eyes and mouth."[3]

Such was the sublime end of the man whom Plato called "the wisest, and justest, and best of all the men whom I have ever known."

II

Jesus and the Joy of Christianity

I doubt the possibility, or propriety, of settling the religion of Jesus Christ in the models of man-made creeds and dogmas. It was a spirit in the life that he laid stress on and taught, if I read aright. I know I see it to be so with me.

The fundamental truths reported in the four gospels as from the lips of Jesus Christ and that I first heard from the lips of my mother are settled and fixed moral precepts with me. I have concluded to dismiss from my mind the debatable wrangles that once perplexed me with distractions that stirred up, but never absolutely settled, anything. I have tossed them aside with the doubtful differences which divide denominations — sweeping them all out of my mind among the non-essentials. I have ceased to follow such discussions or be interested in them.

I cannot without mental reservations assent to long and complicated creeds and catechisms. If the church would ask simply for assent to the Saviour's statement of the substance of the law: "Thou shalt love the Lord thy God with all thy heart, and with all thy soul, and with all thy mind, and thy neighbor as thyself," — that church would I gladly unite with.

— ABRAHAM LINCOLN

H. G. WELLS, THE DISTINGUISHED BRITISH AUTHOR and historian, holds that Western civilization is more indebted to Jesus of Nazareth than to any other personality.

While it is true that a large part of the Christian system

of theological thought stems directly and indirectly from Zoroaster, the central core of the Christian ethical gospel must be credited to the teachings of Jesus and especially to the kind of life he lived.

Modern scholars make a valid distinction between "the religion *of* Jesus" on the one hand and "the religion *about* Jesus" on the other.

The religion *of* Jesus deals almost entirely with the relation of man to his God and his fellowman. The religion *about* Jesus deals primarily with the place of one man, Jesus, in a theological system of thought.

While it is the religion *of* Jesus which we liberals would emphasize today, we do not wish to ignore the immense historic service rendered by the religion *about* him.

If it had not been for the theological dogmas in which the personality of the Galilean prophet was wrapped, there is a strong possibility that you and I today would be without any knowledge or awareness of him.

The beauty of his parables and teachings might have been lost to the world forever.

If the stories of his Virgin Birth, the visit of the Wise Men, his temptations in the wilderness, his physical resurrection from the grave, his ascension to Heaven, and his elevation to the rank of Deity, had not gathered about his name, it is not improbable that the gospel of Jesus would have scarcely survived the generation in which it arose. For the mystical cult of Mithra which was dominant throughout the Roman empire when Jesus was born had most of these attractive theological trappings. Early Christianity was forced by competition with this cult to adopt these trappings in order to make any headway. Even with these advantages Christianity found it a nip and tuck struggle to survive at all. The early Christians were called atheists and traitors, and numerous attempts were made to exterminate them as though they were vermin. We do not mean to suggest that the early Christians consciously adopted the thought patterns of Mithraism in order to compete with it, but merely that those patterns were part of the general cultural environment of the times which few could escape.

What is it then that we owe to Jesus and his religion? There are at least five important ideals and principles we cherish today which can be traced back to his life and influence. He was not the first to enunciate them, but by his gift for literary expression and especially by the power of his own example, he gave them a vitality and reinforcement which they had never had before.

First of all, there is our present high conception of childhood and the place of little children in human society.

Very few of the religious seers and prophets paid much attention to little children in so far as we have any authentic record.

Buddha, for example, ran off from his own child for seven years.

Mohammed did not hesitate to slaughter little children when they got in the way of his crusading armies.

Confucius was kindly to children but in his scheme of society they occupied a very subordinate position. They were to be "seen and not heard."

Even in the Old Testament we find how the prophet Elisha turned with savage fury against the boys and girls who were merely making sport of his physical appearance.

We search the records of all religions in vain to find any incident that begins to compare with the one in which Jesus rebukes his disciples for keeping certain children from obtruding themselves upon his attention; or the one where he places his hand on the head of a little child and declares him to be the greatest in the Kingdom of Heaven; or the incident where he pronounces divine judgment against all those who cause "one of these little ones to stumble."

The Chinese sage, Mo Ti, the Egyptian Pharaoh Akhnaton

and the Buddhist king, Asoka, are the only others in history who seem to have had as high an appreciation of the worth and wisdom of the little child.

However, with respect to our Western civilization, our present orphan asylums, our child labor law, our public nurseries and kindergartens, our societies for the prevention of cruelty to children, and our concern for the wandering and homeless waifs of war-scarred Europe and Asia, can be credited in no small part to the teaching and example of Jesus.

Wherever Christianity has gone, it has tended to lower the infant mortality rate, to lift the social status of little children, and to insist upon special protection for them.

A second ideal we owe to Jesus is our present high conception of womanhood and motherhood.

It is difficult for us to believe that there ever was a time when a woman had no rights she could call her own, when she was looked upon as a mere accessory to the life of man, when she was not even thought to possess a soul.

Orthodox Judaism still insists on the ascendancy of the male over the female, in both the synagogue and society. It is the men who carry on the services of worship.

Mohammedism still regards the woman as much lower in the social scale than the man. Services of worship in this religion are also carried on by men only.

Confucius gave motherhood a high place of dignity within the confines of the home, but outside these confines, a strictly subordinate position.

The laws of orthodox Hinduism, while also giving a dignified status to the mother within the domestic circle, limited her rights to the lifetime of her husband and until recently required that at his death, her life should be offered on his funeral pyre.

Even the Apostle Paul, who did so much to shape the course of Christianity, recommended that women should keep silent in church.

The ideas and ideals of Jesus are in sharp contrast to all such prejudices against women and in favor of men. His sincere sympathy for the woman who was about to be stoned to death because she had lavished her love unwisely; his stern rebuke of the self-righteous who would have taken her life so unmercifully; his unqualified condemnation of the Mosaic law of divorce which made wives the victims of their husbands' whims without redress; his quick defense of the woman who laved costly ointment on his feet; his close friendship with Mary and Martha of Bethany; his tender concern for his own mother at the time of his crucifixion — all these have tended to exalt the world's concept of womanhood and motherhood.

It is not unfair to say that the position of women in Western civilization today — which is steadily improving — would be unthinkable without the original contribution of Jesus. His frank rejection of the double-standard in morality and his firm insistence on the spiritual equality of male and female, will no doubt bring about still greater rights for women than they enjoy even today.

A third ideal which we owe to him is, of course, our high conception of human personality itself. All men and women, according to Jesus even the wayward and the sinful, are precious in the sight of God. As the shepherd leaves the ninety and nine to care for the one sheep that has gone astray; as the father goes forth to welcome home his long absent prodigal son who has wasted his substance in riotous living; as the housewife turns aside from all other concerns to search diligently for the precious coin that has been lost; so in the eyes of the Creator every man, woman and child is precious. The infinite worth of each individual no matter what his social or spiritual status, yes, even his priority over the long cherished institutions of society — this is the sublime teaching of Jesus.

It was he who said, "The Sabbath was made for man, and not man for the Sabbath."

"The kings of the Gentiles exercise lordship over them; and they that exercise authority upon them are called benefactors.

"But ye shall not be so: but he that is greatest among you, let him be as the younger; and he that is chief, as he that doth serve."

.   .   .   .   .

"The spirit of the Lord is upon me, because he hath anointed me to preach the gospel to the poor; he hath sent me to heal the brokenhearted, to preach deliverance to the captives, and recovery of sight to the blind, to set at liberty them that are bruised,

"To preach the acceptable year of the Lord."

Here we have a very fundamental and socially dynamic idea. Who can deny its tremendous leavening power in the past? Who dares to put a limit to its revolutionary possibilities in the future? The contention of Jesus that man is sacred in the eyes of God has brought forth the political doctrine that all governments derive their just powers from the consent of the governed. Give it enough time in which to operate and this idea will undermine the foundations of every totalitarian dictatorship in the world, whether political or religious in character. It will ultimately destroy every form of human exploitation.

In the fourth place, there is the ideal of love as the loftiest and most compelling motive in life. This, too, we owe largely to Jesus in so far as Western civilization is concerned.

Confucius spoke of duty and reverence as the chief motive and so did Lao-tse. Buddha spoke of escape from illusion. Epicurus spoke of seeking pleasure and avoiding pain. Mohammed preached a gospel of submission to the divine will. Zoroaster emphasized the avoidance of hell and eternal punishment.

But Jesus struck the triumphant note of love, although others had struck it before. Mo Ti had done it in China but

the note was smothered in the discord of persecution. To
be mentioned also are Hosea, the Hebrew prophet from
Samaria, and Rabbi Hillel who immediately preceded the
Christian era; also Akhnaton and Asoka.

Jesus, however, sounded the note of love more forcefully
than anyone before, and made it the keynote of his gospel.
"Love," said the late Mahatma Gandhi, "is without doubt
the center and core of the teachings of Jesus." The Aramaic
equivalent of our own word "love" was constantly on his lips.

Several years ago, a Jewish friend, Dr. Meyer Jacobstein,
former congressman, now a consultant on economic affairs in
Washington, D. C., frankly told me that he often wondered
why the Christian religion seemed to be such a joyous and
optimistic religion, why it produced such glad and triumphant music which he thought was a marked characteristic of
the Christian faith as compared with all others, including his
own. He said he had come to the conclusion that it was chiefly
due to the Christian emphasis on love as the great motivation
of life — not fear, not duty, not resignation, not rewards and
punishments, but love — love to God and love to man. It was
the love in Jesus that had produced this contagious joy.

Yes, it is this motive which has produced the radiance of
the Christian saints from Stephen, the first century martyr,
through Francis of Assisi, to Albert Schweitzer, Jane Addams,
and Doctor Grenfell of our own day and generation.

Finally, there is the hope of a righteous ordering of this
world or the doctrine of the Kingdom of Heaven on earth.
This too we owe to Jesus, though he was not the sole origi-
nator of the concept. The great Hebrew prophets had enter-
tained this hope before. Zoroaster proclaimed the coming
of a Messianic reign on earth. Jesus, however, took the idea
and gave it a richer and more definite content. He removed
the violence and intolerance from Zoroaster's concept and
gave immediacy to the nebulous and distant hope of the
Hebrew prophets. He brought the idea down to earth as a

divine state of affairs within the reach of intelligent human beings. "Behold, the Kingdom of Heaven is at hand," he proclaimed.

"Be not therefore anxious, saying, What shall we eat? or, What shall we drink? or, Wherewithal shall we be clothed? For after all these things the Gentiles seek; for your heavenly Father knoweth that ye have need of all these things. But seek ye first the kingdom, and his righteousness; and all these things shall be added unto you."

This earth is a beautiful and bountiful place in which to live. All that is required is understanding and cooperation, one with another, to make it truly a heavenly kingdom. The security and blessedness that each seeks for himself will be found only in the security and blessedness of all. This kingdom, therefore, must start first in the hearts of men as good will and self-discipline before it can be realized in human society — "First the blade, then the ear, then the full corn in the ear."

So important did Jesus consider the hope of a heavenly kingdom on earth that he put it into the prayer which he taught his disciples: "Thy Kingdom come — thy will be done on earth as it is in Heaven."

While Christian churches and temples have repeated this prayer for centuries, its vision of the Heavenly Kingdom was seldom thought of in relation to the life here on earth, but largely to the life hereafter. It is only in recent years that the Christian Church has begun to realize that Jesus meant that this earth was the scene of its realization. The Christian Church is today beginning to compensate for its past neglect by marshalling its prayers and energies as never before around the religion of Jesus, insisting that the time is ripe for the will of God to be done on earth, especially in the sphere of international relations.

Occasionally in the daily press, but more frequently in the religious press, we see pronouncements made and action taken by our churches which indicate an increasing determination on the part of the Christian Church to put the ethical ideas and ideals of Jesus into practical operation as the only hope of salvation for the world.

They are beginning to realize with Bernard Shaw that there is nothing wrong with the religion *of* Jesus except that until recently it has largely been left untried.

It is only the religion *about* Jesus which has hitherto been adequately tried and it is this which has stirred up so much strife in the world, divided Christendom into so many contending fragments and permitted Christian nations to become among the most warlike in history.

It is high time that we turned to the religion *of* Jesus, the religion of the Prince of Peace and gave it at least as fair a test.

There are an increasing number who believe it offers the most practical way out of the present tragic plight of the world.

> O thou great friend to all the sons of men,
>   Who once appeared in humblest guise below,
> Sin to rebuke, to break the captive's chain,
>   And call thy brethren forth from want and woe!
>
> We look to thee: thy truth is still the light
>   Which guides the nations, groping on their way,
> Stumbling and falling in disastrous night,
>   Yet hoping ever for the perfect day.
>
> Yes: thou art still the life; thou art the way
>   The holiest know, — light, life and way of heav'n;
> And they who dearest hope, and deepest pray,
>   Toil by the light, life, way, which thou hast giv'n.

12

Marcus Aurelius and the Stoic Virtues

THE BEST OF ALL RETREATS

Men seek retreats for themselves, houses in the country, sea-shores and mountains; and thou too art wont to desire such things very much. But it is within thy power whenever thou shalt choose to retire into thyself. For nowhere either with more quiet or more freedom from trouble does a man retire than into his own soul, particularly when he has within him such thoughts that by looking into them he is immediately in perfect tranquillity; and I affirm that tranquillity is nothing else than the good ordering of the mind. Constantly then give to thyself this retreat, and renew thyself; and let thy principles be brief and fundamental, which, as soon as thou shalt recur to them, will be sufficient to cleanse thy soul completely, and to send thee back free from all discontent with the things to which thou returnest. . . .

Look within. Within is the fountain of good.

— MARCUS AURELIUS

IN AN AGE OF UNCERTAIN LEADERSHIP, clashing ideologies, and bewildering fears, it is wholesome experience to turn to leaders and thinkers of another age who knew where they were going and why.

Marcus Aurelius, the Roman statesman and Stoic philosopher, was just such a leader. He was a ruler who put politics into the hands of educators instead of education into the hands of politicians, who wrote books instead of censoring them, who abolished corruption instead of conniving in it,

111

who discouraged personal publicity instead of catering to the vulgar taste for hero worship, who not only ruled an empire as well as a city but likewise ruled himself, bringing his passions and ambitions under the control of reason, who amidst the necessary compromises of statesmanship, kept his own soul uncompromised and free and his own reputation unspotted and unstained.

Let me renew for you the story of this man's life. Marcus Aurelius (to be included with Pharaoh Akhnaton and King Asoka among the saintly monarchs of history) was born in the city of Rome, of patrician parents, 121 years after the birth of Christ. His father died when Marcus was only three years old, the child being then transferred to the home of his grandfather, who was more or less prominent in Rome's political affairs.

It was while at the home of this grandfather that the young lad's ability and nobility attracted the attention of Antoninus who was afterwards to become Emperor of Rome and who took such a fancy to Marcus that he later adopted him as his son, bringing him up in his own home, surrounding him with the finest teachers in the city, offering him his own daughter in marriage, introducing him into the mysteries of politics, finally making him his chief adviser and thus paving the way for his ultimate rise to the highest place in the Empire.

Antoninus did a great deal for his adopted son, but the adopted son also did a great deal for his foster father. Indeed it is quite clear that this foster father would never have become emperor at all if it had not been for the son. The reasons for this are too complicated to explain in detail. It is sufficient for our purposes to know that the Emperor Hadrian, the immediate predecessor of Antoninus, had also noticed the ability of the young Aurelius. It so happened that the legal successor to Hadrian's throne at that time was a certain incompetent by the name of Lucius Verus. Fearing to trust the Empire in these hands alone, Hadrian deliberately nominated Antoninus as his immediate successor, stipulating, however, that at the death of Antoninus, Lucius Verus was to share the Roman throne with the brilliant and competent Aurelius. It was therefore to insure the succession of the latter that Antoninus was made emperor at all.

Accordingly, when Antoninus died, the wishes of his predecessor were faithfully carried out. So completely, however, did Marcus Aurelius overshadow his colleague that the incompetent Lucius Verus would have soon been retired to a lower office had it not been for the integrity and generosity of the man who overshadowed him.

Joint rulerships are as likely to be disappointing as joint pastorates. They test the vanity and weakness of human nature as nothing else does. Men can share more easily with one another every possession before that of power and glory. For this reason Julius Caesar could not get along with Mark Antony, nor Saul with David, nor Paul with Barnabas, nor Napoleon with his brothers, nor Theodore Roosevelt with William Howard Taft.

Marcus Aurelius, however, treated Lucius Verus as an equal, refusing to accept any honors at the hands of the Roman Senate until similar honors had first been voted to his colleague. The two emperors appeared together as frequently as convenient. They made a practice of deferring to one another. They made a great success of their common task, although the patience and good nature of the abler man must have been taxed to the uttermost.

Except for one foreign war in which Lucius Verus reaped all the glory and did nothing to earn it, the joint reign of these two emperors may be considered for all practical purposes as the work of Marcus Aurelius alone.

Under his administration, the Roman Empire reached the zenith of its power and grandeur. The domain of Aurelius extended from the Atlantic Ocean to the boundaries of India, from the British Isles to the sands of the Sahara Desert. Commerce and travel were never safer, prosperity and culture never so widespread, education and religion never before so free.

There had been before more peaceful times, it is true, for when Aurelius came to power restless Germanic hordes to the north and east were beginning to make themselves a nuisance if not a menace. The three wars against the Marcomanni which he waged were primarily defensive wars. They were wars to prevent an expanding race from expanding altogether too far. Marcus Aurelius was temperamentally and philosophically opposed to war. He was by nature and training a lover of peace. He was ever trying to reconcile hostile groups and individuals. Like the Pharaoh Akhnaton, he recoiled from the brutalities and cruelties of war. But unlike the Pharaoh, when war needed to be waged to preserve the bounds of Empire, he carried it on efficiently and triumphantly.

Twelve times the title of Conqueror was conferred upon him by the Roman Senate, but there was none of the spirit of the conqueror in his make-up which had actuated so much of the life of Julius Caesar and Alexander the Great.

When the Marcomanni were finally defeated and driven back, Aurelius granted them generous terms of peace and helped them to reconstruct their devastated territory.

His treatment of the slave population of Rome was likewise worthy of admiration. He did not succeed in freeing the slaves like an Abraham Lincoln, but he did enact laws which made it easier for them to purchase their freedom and impossible for those already emancipated to be re-enslaved. It was during his reign that slaves obtained any legal status whatsoever. Before his time, a slave was nothing more than a mere chattel. His master could take his life as though it were the life of a sheep or a cow, or he could sell him for the gladiatorial arena. Marcus Aurelius changed all this and gave the slave the right to appear in court and sue for justice.

He also improved the status of sons and daughters who, until his day, were to all intents and purposes the slaves of their fathers without the social stigma of slaves. The Roman fathers had the power of life and death over their children and could sell them even into slavery if they chose to do so, possessing sole authority over their choice in marriage, ordering their divorce for no reason at all, and entitled to every bit of property they might acquire.

The legal position of wives and mothers under the early emperors was, if possible, even more precarious than that of sons and daughters. Marcus Aurelius changed all this, also, increasing the independence of both women and children to a considerable extent. Many of our laws, today, having to do with domestic rights and duties, with life and property and person, took definite shape under his competent and guiding hand.

It was he who developed the idea of the mortgage and gave it legal sanction. It was he who originated the legal instrument of incorporation. It was he who probably invented the convenience of paying bills by check instead of cash.

One of the great tasks which confronted him when he came to power was the necessity of raising greater revenue without raising the taxes of the common people. He accomplished this by ferreting out the grafters and incompetents and giving Rome one of the most efficient administrations the Empire ever had.

Former rulers had maintained their dignity by magnificent displays of wealth, but Aurelius maintained his dignity by wise and conscientious effort. He cut down the public appropriations for parades and circuses, but he encouraged liberal donations when the river Tiber overflowed its banks with the worst flood in Roman history; likewise, when the Asiatic plague broke out and decimated the life of the city.

In both instances he did not stop at public appropriations but personally supervised the work of reconstruction.

He was outspokenly opposed to gladiatorial combats, but such was their hold on the Roman populace that the most he could do to mitigate this evil was to order large buttons to be attached to the points of the swords, which had the effect of considerably diminishing the number of fatal wounds.

He paid more deference to the Roman Senate than any emperor before him or after. Like Hitler and Mussolini, he could easily have been an absolute dictator, ignoring parliamentary government altogether, if he had chosen to do so. But, instead, he faithfully attended the sessions of the Roman Senate whenever he was in the city, never leaving it when he had once entered until the solemn benediction of dismissal had been pronounced by its presiding officer.

He had several beautiful daughters, for each one of whom he could have secured a wealthy and politically influential husband. Instead he encouraged them to marry men of character and philosophy, these two possessions being considered by him as the highest achievements.

He preached forgiveness of one's enemies, the overcoming of evil with good. When one of his trusted generals in Armenia, Avidius Cassius, turned traitor to him, organizing an insurrection and proclaiming himself emperor, Marcus Aurelius had an opportunity to test his own sincerity. Renouncing the method of assassination, he courageously took up the challenge of battle. But long before the respective armies were near enough for combat, word was brought that Cassius had been slain by his own Chief of Staff. Instead of feeling elated, the emperor was sincerely disappointed. He said that it robbed him of the greatest trophy that a man could win, namely, the pleasure of pardoning one who had sinned against him, the satisfaction of remaining faithful to one who had sought to break the bonds of friendship. There is little question as to how he would have treated Cassius if that man had been taken alive, for he treated the remaining conspirators with leniency, burning the letter that contained their names (without opening it), and publicly forgiving the cities of Antioch and Alexandria which had furnished the rebellious troops.

His wife Faustina was accused of complicity in the plot but Marcus Aurelius steadfastly refused to place any credence in the charge. From all accounts she was wholly unworthy of the adoration which her husband heaped upon her, but he as a rule referred to her as "his sweet and affectionate Faustina." When she died he was filled with grief, building a temple to her memory in the village where she died and founding in her name a refuge for destitute girls in Rome.

The only blot that rests upon his character or his administration, as far as can be discovered, has to do with the three persecutions which took place against the Christians while he was on the Roman throne. It is not our purpose to portray a saint without any faults or shortcomings, nor do we wish to acquit that noble Roman of all responsibility for the death of the eighty to ninety Christians who were killed during his reign. It is only fair to say, however, that the first two persecutions took place without his having a chance to intervene, while only the third was called to his attention in time.

There is no doubt but that Marcus Aurelius was tolerant toward all religions and intended to treat the Christians justly and even mercifully. We must remember, however, that the Christians were not tolerant of other religions at that time and that they were far from being tolerant of the Roman government. They remained an indigestible and fermenting element in the body politic. They refused to serve in the Roman army and navy. They refused to cooperate in Rome's official philanthropies and amusements. They refused to amalgamate with the rest of the citizenship, keeping entirely to themselves and holding their meetings in secret. They were much like some of the subversives in our midst today, capable of martyrdom and physical courage, but on the whole a cantankerous lot suspected of plotting against the government. If the Christians of the twentieth century were anything like the Christians of the second century, they would no doubt be regarded as undesirable citizens worthy of deportation.

It is clear that Roman public opinion looked upon the Christians not merely as religious heretics but as political traitors — a lawless, stubborn, conspiring company who ought to be dealt with most severely. However, to the lasting credit of Marcus Aurelius be it said he did not permit any wholesale government raids to be made. But where there was definite proof of a Christian's active disloyalty, he gave him the benefit of a trial and a final chance to swear allegiance to Rome before inflicting the extreme penalty of the law.

One thing more remains to be said. Throughout his active and varied career, filled as it was with tremendous and exacting responsibilities, interrupted again and yet again by domestic sorrow and persistent attacks of illness, he yet found time to ponder the nature of man, his duties to himself and others, and his relations to the universe. In other words, he found time to philosophize and keep a record of his philosophy.

His book of Meditations, written at first for no human eye but his own, has fortunately been preserved. It is truly a book of profound and sublime wisdom and yet simple and refreshing in its modernity. The entire collection of meditations is worthy of serious study.

Here is what he has to say about man's duty to himself:

Never value anything as profitable to thyself which shall compel thee to break thy promise, to lose thy self-respect, to hate any man, to suspect any man, to act the hypocrite, or to desire anything that requires walls and curtains. . . . Even thy thoughts should be such that if someone should ask thee, "What hast thou on thy mind?" thou mightest with perfect openness answer and at once, "Why, this and that." [1]

Here are his wise counsels about our relations to others:

One thing here is worth a great deal, to pass thy life in truth
and justice, with a benevolent disposition even to liars and
unjust men. . . . As a horse when he has run, a dog when he has
tracked the game, a bee when it has made the honey, so a man
when he has done a good act, does not call out for others to come
and see, but he goes on to another act, as a vine goes on to produce again the grapes in season.[2]

Here is his philosophy of the universe:

For there is one universe made up of all things, and one God
who pervades all things, and one substance, and one law. . . .
Observe constantly that all things take place by change, and
accustom thyself to consider that the nature of the Universe loves
nothing so much as to change the things which are and to make
new things like them. . . . For we are made for co-operation,
like feet, like hands, like eyelids, like the rows of the upper and
lower teeth. . . . We are all working together to one end, some
with knowledge and design, and others without knowing what
they do. . . . But men co-operate after different fashions: and
even those co-operate abundantly, who find fault with what
happens and those who try to oppose it and to hinder it; for the
universe had need even of such men as these.[3]

Marcus Aurelius may not have been the most perfect incarnation of these ideals and principles, but he was surely
the finest product of the Stoic philosophy and the noblest
Roman of whom there is authentic and abundant record.

With unlimited wealth and power at his command, he
lived a life of dignified simplicity. He deserves to be numbered among the saintly characters of all time. He possessed
a quickened conscience, earnestly strove to lift his life to the
level of that conscience, and attained such a measure of
success that his example is still an inspiration to aspiring
humanity. A genius in the field of law and politics, he was
also a genius in the field of character.

A dozen statesman of his intellectual and moral stature
could change the present world outlook from one of fear and
insecurity to one of hope and promise for all mankind.

13

Mohammed and Racial Equality

CHARITY

One came and said to the Prophet: My mother has died, what shall I do for the good of her soul? The Prophet thought of the panting heat of the desert, and he replied: Dig a well, that the thirsty may have water to drink; the man dug a well, and said: This have I done for my mother.

Every good act is charity; giving water to the thirsty is charity, removing stones and thorns from the road is charity, smiling in your brother's face is charity.

A man's true wealth is the good he does in this world; when he dies, mortals will ask what property he left behind him; but angels will ask him: What good deeds hast thou sent before thee?

. . . .

There is no better ruler than Wisdom, no safer guardian than Justice, no stronger sword than Right, no surer ally than Truth.

— MOHAMMEDAN SCRIPTURES

LONG BEFORE MOST OF US were awake, words with the following meaning were proclaimed from a thousand minarets and more throughout the world:

Allahu Akbar! God is great, God is great,, God is great!
I bear witness that there is no god but God!
I bear witness that there is no god but God!
I bear witness that Mohammed is the apostle of God!

120

I bear witness that Mohammed is the apostle of God!
Come hither to prayers!
Come hither to prayers!
Come hither to salvation!
Come hither to salvation!
God is great! There is no other god but God!
Prayer is better than sleep! [1]

With the exception of the phrase, "Prayer is better than sleep," which, of course, is said only in the early morning, this call to worship can be heard five times a day, every day in the week from every Moslem minaret throughout the world, as the muezzin, the Moslem crier, faces the North, the East, the South and the West.

Measured by the mark he has made upon the world, and by the changes he has wrought in the course of human history, Mohammed is truly one of the great personalities of all time.

His religion today numbers two hundred and fifty million adherents,[2] more than at any other period before, and is the fastest growing religion in the world at the present time, expanding at the rate of two hundred and fifty thousand converts each year.

Mohammed did not possess the saintliness of Jesus, Buddha or Mo Ti, nor the philosophical discernment of Confucius, Lao-tse, or Zoroaster. He is to be compared with such men as Julius Caesar and Genghis Khan, with the King Davids and the Emperor Constantines of religion. Someone has said he had,

> The monarch mind, the mystery of commanding,
>   The birth-hour gift, the art Napoleon,
> Of wielding, moulding, gathering, welding, banding,
>   The hearts of thousands till they moved as one.[3]

He was one of the four founders of new religions who lived to see the faith he founded attain a large measure of success; the other three being Zoroaster and Buddha and Mary Baker

Eddy. Most of the others died discouraged in heart and apparently defeated. But not so with Mohammed. Before he passed from the stage of earthly life, the entire population of Arabia was sitting at his feet and within one hundred and twenty-five years thereafter, his spiritual domain extended from the Indian Ocean to the Straits of Gibraltar.

Such a personality is certainly worthy of our serious consideration and study. He and Moses are the only ones among the great founders of religion who have never been deified. The fierce opposition of both to all forms of idolatry tended to discourage such a development.

Mohammed, or Ubal-Kassim, was born in the city of Mecca about 570 A.D. Ubal Kassim was his real name. Mohammed was the religious name by which he was called by his followers in later years, Mohammed meaning "the Praised One," as Christ means "the Anointed One," and as Buddha means "the Enlightened One."

Mohammed lost both his father and mother before he was six years of age, and was brought up by his grandfather, and then by a fond uncle who had grand ambitions for his adopted son, but no means to carry them out. Consequently, Mohammed had to go to work at an early age in order to earn his own livelihood.

He became a camel driver at fourteen and went off with trading caravans as far away as Egypt and Palestine. In Palestine, he learned about the religious disputes between Jews and Christians.

At twenty-two he went to work for Kadijah, the widow of a wealthy merchant of Mecca, and at twenty-five, married her even though she was fifteen years his senior. She it was who became the greatest inspiration in his life. She relieved him of the necessity of earning a livelihood and thus enabled him to indulge his speculative and meditative nature.

Tall, broad-shouldered and handsome, "the well-dressed product of a wise and prudent marriage," Mohammed used to sit in the market place of Mecca, discussing, hour after hour, all sorts of questions but especially those having to do with religion.

In the center of the city was the towering Kaaba, a cubical structure with niches in it for the images of three hundred and sixty gods and goddesses. In the southeast corner is the famous black stone. This sacred building reminded Mohammed of how his father as a small lad had once been brought to this center of worship to be offered up as a living sacrifice to one of these gods (as Isaac was brought by Abraham to Mount Moriah), and was only saved from a terrible fate, at the last moment, by the payment of an exorbitant sum on the part of his relatives. Mohammed, with this story fresh in his mind, recoiled in horror at the continuation of this monstrous custom and became convinced that there was no sense to it, and that all idol worship was utterly devoid of spiritual meaning and significance.

From time to time he took refuge in a desert cave to meditate. At the age of forty, he began to see visions and hear voices in the cave. He claimed that the angel Gabriel appeared again and again in these visions and finally revealed to him the idea of one God — Allah, the supreme power behind all life. The angel commissioned Mohammed to be his prophet to preach the duty of everyone in Heaven and on Earth to bow in submission to Allah's will.

Although he could neither read nor write, he dictated to friends and relatives an eloquent account of what he saw and heard in his desert cave. Later on these records were gathered together and constitute the Koran, the Bible of this religion, one hundred and fourteen chapters in all — each chapter being the record of a separate vision.

His first, and most enthusiastic, convert was his wife, Kadijah. She constantly gave him every encouragement and reassurance, ministering to his every need with infinite tenderness and patience. Some men can be loved into greatness — others, like Socrates and Confucius, require more drastic treatment. At any rate, from this point on, Mohammed began to preach his new religion with increasing fervor and self-confidence.

For ten years he labored in his home city of Mecca against great odds and with only meager success. The people of that city were too fond of their idols to desert them for Allah. The idols could be seen and touched, whereas belief in Allah put too much strain on the human imagination. Besides, the idols attracted great hordes of pilgrims to the city, and this was certainly good for business. Therefore the converts to the faith of Allah were at first very few in number, and, for the most part, people of no account in the community.

At one time the Prophet and his followers were strictly confined by official decree to a narrow section of Mecca where an attempt was made to starve them into submission. Mecca being a Holy City, it was sacrilege to take human life directly within the city limits. But there was no law against death by starvation. This method failing, however, to achieve the desired results, the city officials, urged on by those who had vested interests in the worship of idols, finally decided to resort to outright assassination to get rid of the obnoxious prophet. But Mohammed got wind of the plot and fled in the nick of time to his secret cave in the desert, ultimately finding more permanent refuge in the neighboring city of Medina, to which his friends had fled before him. This flight of Mohammed is called the Hegira and from it the whole Mohammedan world dates its calendar — the day corresponding to July 15, 622 A.D. At Medina the prophet was given a wild and enthusiastic reception by its citizens who turned out en masse to greet him and at once proclaim him ruler of the city. It was at Medina that he changed the direction of the face in prayer from Mecca to Jerusalem. He did this in order to enlist the support of the many Jews in the city and the many Christians in the neighboring city of Najran, who, he hoped, would accept him as a successor to their own prophets. Failing in this he finally changed the direction back again from Jerusalem to Mecca and proceeded to persecute the Jews for their reluctance to be converted.

It was at Medina that the faithful Kadijah died. This bereavement brought about a great change in Mohammed. In short order he took unto himself more than the legal number of wives, which was four, most of them the widows of officers recently slain in battle. He justified his conduct by claiming special sanction from Heaven.

It was at Medina that the prophet organized bandit gangs, whose business it was to rob passing caravans to obtain funds for his missionary enterprises. He even allowed this to be done during the month of Holy Pilgrimage. He called his robbery taxation and his bandit gangs tax collectors. It depends on who is telling the story!

It was at Medina that he changed from a persecuted prophet to a persecuting one. The former idealist took on some of the characteristics of a charlatan. Islam (which means submission to the will of God) was transformed from a religion of moral suasion to one of force and plunder, and from one of rich spiritual integrity to one of low political expediency.

Eight years after the flight from Mecca, Mohammed was able to put himself at the head of an army of ten thousand Arabians to return and lay siege to the city.

When Jesus returned to his home city of Nazareth, he returned to comfort the broken-hearted and heal "the maimed, and the halt, and the blind." But when Mohammed returned to Mecca, he went with a huge army and instead of healing the maimed, and the halt, and the blind, and the broken-hearted, he succeeded in increasing their misery. He finally conquered the city. One by one the various nearby villages and tribes capitulated to his authority, all accepting his new faith outright or at least paying reluctant tribute for its support. His personal and political enemies were ruth-lessly exterminated and eventually he had everything his own way.

He died at the age of sixty-two — ten years after his flight from Mecca — when he was about to measure his strength with the forces of Rome. Death came with very little warn-ing. It was probably an attack of typhoid fever. When he knew his hour had come, he insisted upon going to a nearby mosque, so weak he could barely stand. But he did manage to say:

Moslems! If I have wronged any of you, here am I to answer for it. If I owe aught to anyone, all I may happen to possess belongs to you.[4]

One man claimed the prophet owed a small debt and it was there and then paid. Mohammed was carried home and died a few hours later.

Few men in history have achieved so big a triumph in so short a time — a sickly orphan at the age of six; a poorly paid camel driver at fourteen; the mere husband of a wealthy widow at twenty-five; a neurotic visionary at forty; a despised and hunted fanatic, fleeing for his life at fifty-two — but, ten years more and all Arabia was at his feet, hailing him as the founder of a new religion and the prophet of the only one and true God. This, in brief, is the story of Mohammed, whose very name is prophesied in both our Old and New Testament, according to Moslem interpretation.

It is the story of a man who was at one time undoubtedly gentle, high-minded, even idealistic, filled with compassion for his fellow men and honestly convinced that he had been commissioned from on high to spread an important and liber-ating gospel; but who, later on, subordinated every ethical consideration to the achievement of the ends he sought, re-sorting to trickery, treachery, robbery, battle, murder and sudden death to further what he fanatically believed to be the will of Allah.

In Sura XVII of the Koran, he had said,

Invite men into the way of thy Lord by wisdom and mild exhortation . . . if ye suffer wrong patiently, verily this will be better for the patient. . . . Let there be no violence in religion.[5]

But, unfortunately, in Sura VIII of the same Koran he had said,

Slay the infidel *if he attacks you* and will not let you practice your religion. . . . If they desist from opposing you, what is already past shall be forgiven them. But if they return to attack you, the like shall be inflicted on them. Therefore fight against them until there be no opposition in favor of idolatry and the religion be wholly God's.[6]

This is the scripture which Mohammed himself took the more seriously while he lived and which his followers took even more seriously after the prophet's death. Instead of waiting until attacked, they found it better to do the attacking. This sanction of force and violence is no small part of the spiritual legacy which he bequeathed to mankind. Surely, in this respect Mohammed stands on a moral plane that is much below that of Confucius, Mo Ti, Lao-tse, Buddha or Jesus. Only Zoroaster shared his zeal in the use of the sword.

Fortunately, the ethics and the practice of the Moslem faith today are far superior to the harsh example of its founder. It is true that Islam in the past has been guilty of cruel wars of conquest but so has Christian civilization. Witness the Crusades, the One Hundred Years' War and the World Wars One and Two. It is true that the Moslem world has been divided into quarreling sects and denominations, but so has Christianity. It is true that there was once a sect of Moslems who justified secret murder in the name of religion, calling themselves Assassins, from which our own word is derived. But let us not overlook the Borgias who did much worse and for years presided upon the papal throne of Christendom.

Several charges against Islam can be justly made, such as

its easy tolerance of legal polygamy and its exaltation of man's place in society over that of woman. But there are certain other values which can be signalized to its everlasting credit.

In the first place, the Moslem faith held aloft the torch of science at a time when Christian Europe was groping its way through the Dark Ages. Someone has said: "If there is one thing that deserves to rank in sacredness with the blood of the martyrs, it is the ink of the scholars."

The Koran pays the following tribute to knowledge. It says:

Acquire knowledge because he who acquires it in the way of the Lord performs an act of piety. Knowledge enables its possessor to distinguish what is forbidden from what is not; it lights the way to heaven; it is our friend in the desert, our society in solitude, our companion when bereft of friends; it guides us to happiness; it sustains us in misery; it is our ornament in the company of friends; it serves as armor against our enemies. With knowledge the servant of God rises to the height of goodness and to a noble position, associates with the sovereigns of this world and attains to the perfection of happiness in the next.[7]

The Moslem world took the torch of science from the hands of the Greeks and Romans, and kept it burning until we of the Western world caught its flame.

Moslem scholars preserved for us the finest translations of Plato's and Aristotle's writings.

They developed the science of mathematics, giving to the Western world the Arabic numerals and the decimal system of notation.

They developed trigonometry, inventing the sine and co-sine, the tangent and cotangent. Algebra can be credited to their account.

They discovered the use of the pendulum and made clocks long before they were made in Europe.

Their materia medica was far and away ahead of everything in Christian Europe at that time — fully five hundred years ahead. They used anesthetics and performed major operations.

Until the seventeenth century, Christian Europe seldom bathed. The sanitary habits even of the nobles as well as of the common people were appalling. There were no hospitals, no sewage system, no paved streets, no public libraries, but in the ninth and tenth centuries, the Moslem cities of Baghdad, Damascus and Cordova were great cities of culture. Cordova alone had three hundred public baths besides those in private homes. It had well-paved streets, fine shops, vast libraries and more than a dozen colleges.[8]

In astronomy the Moslems made great strides calculating the angle of the ecliptic and the precession of the equinoxes with scientific precision.

In chemistry they made a considerable headway discovering such substances as alcohol, potash, nitrate of silver and sulphuric acid. They knew the secret of dyeing and manufactured paper without which the printing press of Europe would have been of no avail.

The second achievement which goes to their credit is the fact that they held aloft the torch of monotheism at a time when Christian Europe had sunk back into the darkness of pagan polytheism. They took their light from the candle of Judaism and kept it burning until that candle could be set on a hill once more for all the world to see, and from which several religious liberal groups derived the light which they have now held aloft for more than a century and a half.

No matter what we may think of Mohammed's Allah in certain respects, surely one God is preferable to 360 or even to three in one.

A monistic conception of the universe does less violence to human reason than any other and prepares the way for the ideal of one brotherhood of the human race.

It certainly tends to discourage the degrading and befuddling practice of idolatry in the world.

Whatever the mistakes of Islam, it has never made the mistake of raising a human being to the rank of Deity.

Mohammed definitely repudiated the idea that he was more than a man, and his followers have respected his views on this matter.

On this point, we religious liberals regard them as friends and kindred spirits.

In the third place, the Moslems have held aloft the torch of race equality. It knows no caste or color bar. All its professions, schools, hospitals and other institutions have been open to everyone from the very beginning of the faith without regard to the accident of birth, social status or national origin. Moslems do not merely talk race equality, they practice it. This is one of the chief reasons why it has made and is still making such astonishing headway in the Near East, the Far East, in China, India, Indonesia and Africa.

It is also one of the more democratic religions in that it repudiates all intermediaries between man and God, being entirely free of a priesthood and any ecclesiastical hierarchy. It is not a one-day-in-the-week religion, but every day — five times a day — the Mohammedan can kneel on his prayer mat, in his home and office, or in the field. Islam does not even take up a collection, its minarets and mosques being supported by taxation. In America we prefer supporting religion by freewill offerings.

Finally, it is only fair to point out that this faith, which in its early history was clearly intolerant, has its more tolerant aspects. Its Koran teaches that the prophets of all religions are to be treated with respect, their names never to be mentioned without the prefix of "His Holiness."

All that it asks is that Mohammed be recognized as one of God's prophets and not necessarily the chief among them. For the Koran declares:

There is no distinction between Prophets. . . . Say we believe in God and that which hath been sent down to us, and that which was sent down to Abraham, and Ishmael, and Isaac, and Jacob, and the tribes, and that which was delivered to Moses and Jesus and the Prophets from their Lord; we make no distinction between any of them. (Koran VII)

Those who . . . would make a distinction between God and His Apostles and say we believe in some of the prophets and reject others of them . . . these are really unbelievers. (Koran IV) [9]

It would be difficult to find a more liberal or truly fair statement in the teachings of any religion. It is this broad-minded inclusiveness which is being emphasized today far more than at any time before, while the intolerant aspects are being deliberately played down. For this reason, Islam is today once more on the march, but it is a spiritual advance that is being achieved, and not a military one. It is now the good in this religion which constitutes the greatest challenge to Christianity. Therefore, we may view the contest that lies ahead with less misgivings and with more hope for the future welfare of all mankind.

14

Francis of Assisi and the Lady Poverty

O Lord, our Christ, may we have thy mind and thy spirit; make us instruments of thy peace; where there is hatred, let us sow love; where there is injury, pardon; where there is discord, union; where there is doubt, faith; where there is despair, hope; where there is darkness, light; and where there is sadness, joy. O divine Master, grant that we may not so much seek to be consoled as to console; to be understood, as to understand; to be loved, as to love; for it is in giving that we receive, it is in pardoning that we are pardoned, and it is in dying that we are born to eternal life. Amen.

— FRANCIS OF ASSISI

FRANCIS OF ASSISI, early canonized as one of the great saints of the Roman Catholic Church, has been long since recognized by the non-Roman Catholic world as one of the great saints of all time. He was truly one of the most romantic figures ever to grace this planet, whose career was filled with throbbing human interest, the bare account of which reads like a thrilling piece of fiction.

To understand his relevance to our own age, we must first understand the civilization of which he was a part — a civilization based on a crumbling feudalism, whose people lived

132

in semi-independent city states where the merchant and the business man were just beginning to rise to some measure of social respectability, where everybody, rulers and ruled alike, acknowledged the supreme authority of the Roman pontiff, where all churches were united because there was only one Church, and that Church at the zenith of its temporal power and glory; and where a flat earth and a definitely located Heaven and Hell constituted the cosmology of both learned and unlearned with no doubt cast upon its accuracy by anyone worthy of notice.

Into this world, a soul was born who did much to sweeten it, to illuminate it, and to redeem it.

His name was John Bernardone — the son of a rich merchant who carried on a flourishing silk business in the little town of Assisi in central Italy.

John Bernardone, who was afterwards to bear the name of Francis because of his fondness for singing the songs of France, was born in the year 1182 and died in 1226, at the age of forty-four.

There were some at that time who referred to him as "Poor Francis, God's fool, the gentle imbecile, the altruistic lunatic." Others said, "What a pity that one with his inheritance of wealth should have been so deluded as to throw away advantages which nearly everyone else greatly coveted! What a shame that a man of such promise should have become such a victim of hallucination as to deny himself even the joys of life." Many questioned the soundness of his mind.

Such pity, however, was wholly gratuitous. Probably few people in all the world, even of those who had lived twice his age ever got so much real joy and happiness out of life as he.

Let us look at a few snapshots of his adventurous career — snapshots that picture him in the more important of the many roles which he succeeded in playing in his short life.

First of all, let us direct our attention to St. Francis before he became a saint, to the youthful reveller, the prodigal son of a proud and indulgent father who takes delight in hearing the neighbors say of his boy, "There goes the merchant's son who lives like a prince."

From the age of seventeen until he was twenty-seven, Francis spent his father's money lavishly and even recklessly in midnight banquets and riotous dances, travelling through the streets of Assisi in the small hours of the morning, serenading his numerous ladyloves in company with other youthful revellers, living a life of idleness and luxury, and only visiting his father's place of business on occasion to see how far he might dare to go in his life of prodigality and extravagance.

Tiring of revelry, he looks for something more adventurous.

We behold him next as a crusading knight, fighting for the liberty of his city against the oppressions of a greedy feudal lord.

As a soldier he is brave and daring. He is captured and languishes in prison, only to be released and to unite himself to the army of a wandering duke who has lost his dukedom and is trying to recover it. Francis equips himself with the finest armor of his day and rides forth to fight once more. But before he rides very far, something happens to him. We do not know exactly what, but, like Socrates on the field of battle and Paul on the road to Damascus, this soldier has a vision of the heavens opening before him, and he hears a strange, authoritative voice. The voice rebukes him for wasting his strength in following such an unworthy master as an earthly duke, and bids him return at once to Assisi, there to serve the Lord of Lords and King of Kings.

In simple faith, Francis obeys this voice and returns to Assisi; and there he reads once more the story of the rich young ruler and is tremendously impressed. For the last time he consents to preside at a banquet of his friends.

Later on, when his joyous guests parade the streets, dancing and singing after their boisterous custom, they notice that their host remains behind, wrapped in deep and serious meditation. They taunt him with thinking of taking a wife.

"Yes," he replies, "I have resolved to take a wife. But a wife far nobler, richer and more beautiful than any of you know anything about. It is the Lady Poverty."

A new ideal has flashed before his eyes to which he will now consecrate the rest of his days. It is neither revelry nor knighthood — but Christian poverty.

The third picture, which we have of him is as a champion of this ideal. We who live in an age which worships at the shrine of prosperity and efficiency, far from the easy-going but hospitable life of first century Galilee and thirteenth century Italy, we find it very difficult indeed to understand poverty as an ideal in any shape or degree.

To Francis, however, as to Jesus, poverty was neither a hardship nor a sacrifice, but a prerequisite of the joyous and abundant life. There was nothing of barren asceticism in the philosophy of either. "Deliberate poverty," Francis declared, "frees men from the anxieties and tyrannies that always go with possessions. It emancipates their minds and liberates their spirits." "Sufficient unto the day is the evil thereof," he quoted. Men are grievously burdened with the cares of property on every hand. They are literally wearing themselves out with the lust for accumulation and the responsibilities of ownership. If you want to live the highest and fullest life possible, he preached, go, and sell whatsoever that thou hast, and give to the poor; and do not allow yourself ever again to become encumbered with any more property so long as you live. The more things you acquire, the more things you will want. Increasing one's possessions is the surest way of decreasing one's peace of mind. Live from hand to mouth. Satisfy your daily needs by daily labor. If there is a surplus, get rid of it before another dawn, by sharing with those who do not have enough. If you are lacking, do not hesitate to ask of others for their surplus. For men are all children of one heavenly Father and therefore members of one family and what belongs to one belongs to all.

Francis, as you see, was something of a communist, but not of the modern variety, of course. To him all property was an inconvenience and a nuisance. Not only did he eschew private ownership of wealth, but also common ownership as well.

The Order of Little Brothers and the Order of Poor Clares, both of which he founded, were not allowed at first to hold any property, either as individuals or as a group.

The other monastic orders of that day, Francis observed, had grown fat with prosperity and had lost their souls and their spiritual influence. To guard against this blunder was his first objective.

Accordingly, he fought with fanatical zeal all efforts within and without his order to corrupt it with the acquisition of property of any kind. Whatever you and I may think of his sociology, we certainly cannot question his sincerity. Probably no man ever existed who was so covetous of wealth as he was covetous of poverty.

The fourth picture is of St. Francis as a builder of churches and men.

A voice that seems to come from Heaven bids him turn his attention to the churches falling into ruins. With his own hands he reconstructs the walls of many a dilapidated edifice or wayside shrine. With tireless zeal and patience he summons others to help him.

The heavenly voice becomes a great deal clearer, and the injunction to build is given a wider meaning. The Church becomes identified with the larger interests of mankind, and Francis becomes a builder of humanity.

Like a conquering army, he and his little band of brothers

attack one village after another — not with the weapons of war, but with the implements of peace and goodwill.

They patch the roofs of the houses of the poor. They clean the sewers and dig drains and ditches. They plant gardens and fruit-trees for others to reap the harvest. They nurse the sick and the aged. They visit the lepers and build huts for their protection. They teach the little children games and sports and take time to romp and play with them. They help the farmers at harvest time to gather in their crops and thresh their grain. They fill the highways and byways with their happy songs and merry laughter.

Barefooted in summertime, and often in winter, simply clad in rough grey garments at all times, with leathern girdles about their waists, this army of joyous troubadours marches triumphantly forward — from one victory to another — leaving behind an aftermath of contented homes, sanitary streets, reconstructed countrysides and transformed personalities.

Not one penny do they levy as tribute. Not one penny do they demand as compensation. All that they will accept is the simplest fare and the humblest shelter as a freewill offering from those who have it to give.

At their head marches the gracious Francis, round of face, sweet and sonorous of voice, above the average in height, with black eyes, black hair and classic features, his teeth even and white — handsome and magnetic with a countenance filled with love and hope and cheer and courage.

No wonder the people hear him gladly. He himself is gladness personified and joy incarnate. Not only does he have a passionate love for human beings of every description and condition, but he is in love with all of life.

As a lover of nature we next see him. The wolf and the ass he calls his brothers. The buds and the insects he calls his sisters. And even the grass and the flowers and the trees and clouds and rivers are his trusted friends and close advisors. Long before Darwin and Wallace announce their startling discoveries, Francis instinctively recognizes his kinship with all the lower forms of life.

How many of us who intellectually accept the logic of evolution actually feel its spiritual implications?

Francis is said to have preached a sermon to the birds who listened attentively and then sang an anthem in his honor; and to have lectured a wolf, actually persuading the beast to give up his ferocity in exchange for board and lodging.

Whether these legends are disbelieved in whole or in part, they show at least that their subject was a genuine communicant of nature. Otherwise these legends would never have grown around his personality.

The next picture is that of Francis as a foe of feudalism.

Realizing that his Order of Little Brothers and his Order of Poor Clares were quite beyond the reach of ordinary human nature, he founded a third Order which did not involve the abandonment of property, but which did involve the renunciation of solemn oaths of allegiance to anyone and the carrying of offensive weapons. The feudal lords objected strenuously because their very existence depended upon these props. But the Pope protected Francis in his great reform.

In the second place, everyone who joined this order was required to pay dues to a common fund which was to be used for emergency purposes in cases of accident or sudden changes in fortune. This provision helped the serfs who joined to keep from getting further in debt to their lords and thus postponing indefinitely their final liberation.

In the third place, every applicant was required to make a will within three months. This was to prevent whatever property a serf did own from falling into the hands of his lord who could otherwise legally claim it if the serf died intestate.

All these measures tended to undermine the very foundation of feudalism and to hasten the final crash of the super-
structure — for all of which we can honestly give some
measure of credit to St. Francis.

There are only two more pictures in our brief album of
his life.

One of them shows St. Francis as a courageous missionary
to the Sultan. History has seldom recorded such an example
of supreme audacity as was his, when, unarmed and unaccompanied except by one faithful disciple, he set out to conquer
the infidel Mohammedan by converting him to Christianity.
There he goes, bravely crossing that river in Egypt which
separates the armed camp of Christendom from that of the
Moslem hordes, seeking an audience with none other than
the Sultan himself, resolved to win him to the Cross of Christ
or die in the attempt. He is taken captive, cruelly beaten
and bruised, but finally given the audience he requests. The
Sultan receives him with compassion and gracious courtesy,
but, of course, declines to be converted.

St. Francis then begs for a chance to prove his faith by
dying for it, but the Sultan grimly shakes his head. He likes
this strange Christian too much to let him die and so returns
him to his coreligionists in perfect safety. The messenger is
received but not the message.

You and I may smile at the simplicity and innocence of
this unsophisticated saint. We may even question his intelligence and emotional balance, but we cannot doubt his
moral courage or his spiritual consecration.

He reminds us of Henry Ford and his Peace Ship — and
how that industrialist sought to get the soldiers out of the
trenches by a certain Christmas during the first World War
— and miserably failed.

He should remind us also of the courage of Napoleon, who,
on his escape from the Island of Elba, fared forth to meet
the army of the king of France alone. Baring his breast to

the guns of his captors, Napoleon dared them to shoot. Instead of surrendering to them, he commanded them to surrender to him, and succeeded by the very audacity of his faith.

Perhaps the mission of St. Francis to the Sultan was not so foolish after all. Given a slightly different setting, he might have been successful. At any rate, the world can afford to entertain a few more fools like St. Francis.

The final portrait of our hero shows him a victim of crucifixion.

There he kneels in prayer with nail holes in his hands and feet, with thorn prints on his brow and bleeding gashes in his breast. It is whispered that he obtained these stigmata by meditating on the crucified figure of his beloved Christ.

Psychologists tell us that such phenomena are not at all impossible — however improbable — when such emotions as St. Francis possessed are taken into consideration. Many moderns, however, are inclined to doubt their authenticity altogether.

Let us accept them as symbolic of what ecclesiasticism finally did to Francis. And what it generally does to humanity's purest spirits.

For, whatever it does to their physical bodies, it ever seeks to crown their faith with thorns, to mangle their finer thoughts and to nail their spiritual hands and feet to the cross of dogma and distortion.

The beautiful spirit of St. Francis was finally crucified — the victim of priestcraft and obscurantism.

The rules about his order owning property in common were changed even before his death by those above him in authority over his own vehement protest. His Little Brothers were eventually showered with gifts and in time became so corrupted by wealth that the original purpose of the Order was entirely lost sight of. The Franciscans finally became almost as parasitical and overbearing as the other religious orders. And then to add sentimentality to sacrilege, the semi-emasculated founder of the order was duly canonized as a saint. Such is the usual procedure of ecclesiastical strategy.

Would to Heaven that St. Francis were living today to become a wholesome antidote to the crass materialism and violence of this age, to cleanse our social drains and sewers, to heal our spiritual leprosy, to cheer our flagging moral forces and to challenge the present armed impasse between the East and West with his sublime faith in the divinity of the human soul!

Would to Heaven that his sweet simplicity, his warm human compassion, his joyous spirit and indomitable courage might be reincarnated again and yet again!

15

Baha'u'llah and World Federation

> We desire but the good of the world and the happiness of the nations; yet they deem us a stirrer up of strife and sedition worthy of bondage and banishment; that all nations should become one in faith and all men as brothers; that the bonds of affection and unity between the sons of men should be strengthened; that diversity of religion should cease, and differences of race be annulled. . . . What harm is there in this? . . . Yet so it shall be; these fruitless strifes, these ruinous wars shall pass away, and the "Most Great Peace" shall come. . . . Is not this that which Christ foretold? . . . Yet do we see your kings and rulers lavishing their treasures more freely on means for the destruction of the human race than on that which would conduce to the happiness of mankind. These strifes and this bloodshed and discord must cease, and all men be as one kindred and one family. . . . Let not a man glory in this, that he loves his country; let him rather glory in this, that he loves his kind.
>
> — BAHA'U'LLAH

ON THE SOUTHWESTERN SHORES of Lake Michigan, in the Chicago suburb of Wilmette, can be seen the dome of a towering temple that dominates the scene for miles in all directions.

It is "a thing of beauty and a joy forever." It has been compared to the Taj Mahal of India but nothing quite like

142

it has ever been seen before. Its architecture is unique, for into its construction has gone designs from the Egyptian, Greek, Romanesque, Arabic, Gothic, Renaissance and modern schools of architecture, together with the characteristic symbols of the major religions of the world, all artfully combined into one harmonious whole.

This impressive temple has been presented to America as a gift from the disciples of Baha'u'llah throughout the world, to symbolize the oneness of the human race and the unity behind all religions.

When the temple is finally completed (work was begun on it over thirty years ago, and it will probably take another year to finish it) it will include a hospital and dispensary, a school for orphan children, a hospice, a college for higher scientific education and beautiful gardens and fountains between the outlying buildings and the temple.

Already its beauty is breathtaking, and if you have not already seen it, you have an exalting experience in store for you.

In the year 1892, there passed away in a Turkish penal colony at the foot of Mount Carmel in Palestine, one of the bravest spirits, one of the broadest minds, one of the noblest characters who ever graced this planet.

Today several millions of people throughout the world hail this person as the Hope of World Peace and the Savior of all Mankind. These people can be found in no less than eighty-eight countries and among all creeds and races, about half of them to be found in Persia.

Baha'u'llah, in the judgment of many, possessed the tenderness of St. Francis, the courage of Socrates, the meekness of Moses, the sanity of Confucius, the missionary vigor of Mohammed, the moral majesty of Isaiah, the compassion of Buddha and the saintliness of Jesus.

This sounds like extravagant praise and you may reasonably question whether any such individual ever lived. But there is overwhelming evidence that such an individual did live and lived for seventy-five years, and under such trying conditions that if there had been any weaknesses in his mind or character, they were bound to be disclosed. But thus far, not even the enemies and persecutors of this man have ventured to say a word against his character.

Baha'u'llah, or Mirza Hussein Ali, was born in Tehran, the capital city of Iran, on November 12, 1817. Mirza Hussein Ali was his real name, although Baha'u'llah was the name by which he came to be called in later years. Baha'u'llah means "the Glory of Allah" just as the name of the prophet Jeremiah means "the Glory of Jehovah."

The family of Baha'u'llah was one of wealth and political distinction, many of its members having occupied important positions in the civil and military services of the government. His father was the Minister of State for many years.

Strange as it may seem with such a background, Baha'u'llah never attended school or college. What little teaching he received was given at home. Nevertheless, even as a child he displayed a wisdom and knowledge far beyond his years. People were naturally drawn to him. He was a great lover of out-of-door life, spending most of his time in the public gardens or in the fields and forest.

When he was twenty-two years of age, his father died, leaving him the management of an extensive family estate and the responsibility of caring for his younger brothers and sisters. The government of Persia or Iran as it is now called, invited him to succeed to his father's position as Minister of State, as was then the custom, but he declined the position. Instead he gave himself to the cause of religion, and this is how it came about.

In 1844, there appeared in Persia a radiant youth known as the Bab, who proclaimed the coming of a mighty educator who was to quicken the minds, unify the hearts and remold the customs of all mankind and bring peace and understanding throughout the world.

After six years of heroic and ardent missionary activity by which the Mohammedan faith in Persia was rent in twain, the Bab became the victim of fanatical persecution and was publicly executed. The year was 1850.

It was at this critical juncture that Baha'u'llah stepped forward to champion the cause of the fallen leader. Considering the amount of public furore, it was not only a brave but almost a rash thing to do. He traveled widely and began to proclaim that the New Age prophesied by the Bab was at hand — the new age of universal brotherhood and universal peace. The spirit of God was about to descend upon all nations and revive the spiritual life of all peoples. A new cycle in history was about to begin and a new religious approach was needed to usher it in.

The orthodox Mohammedan faith was not adequate to the situation. Neither was Christianity nor Judaism, nor any of the other ceremonial and creed-encrusted religions. A fresh and dynamic religious approach was called for. This was dangerous doctrine, of course, dangerous to the Mohammedan faith, at any rate, and the political state then existing.

On a trumped-up charge of treason, Baha'u'llah and his followers were arrested and thrown into prison. Eighty of them were tortured and then put to death at once. In the course of the next few years, twenty thousand in all suffered martyrdom. The life of Baha'u'llah was spared because of his distinguished family background, but he himself was brutally treated, his property was confiscated and he was sentenced to life imprisonment. After spending four years in a dungeon in his native city of Tehran, he was transferred to Baghdad, then to Constantinople, then to Adrianople and finally confined for life in a desolate penal colony at the foot of Mount Carmel in Palestine.

During all these forty years of incarceration, not one word of complaint or vindictiveness escaped his lips that was recorded by either his friends or his persecutors. Under the most trying circumstances, he maintained a serene spirit and a dignified manner, and achieved a radiant personality. In his later years, he was allowed to receive delegations of visitors.

He wrote incessantly, and sent letters not only to his immediate followers, but to many important people throughout the world.

He addressed the Pope beseeching him to purify the Roman Catholic church and lead the way to a better understanding among the world religions.

He wrote to the German Kaiser and the French Emperor, Napoleon III, warning them about the political consequences of war.

He sent an urgent letter to the Russian Czar, imploring him to call a world congress of the nations to establish an international court of justice.

He wrote public letters to the American people urging this country to lead the way to universal peace.

He dispatched like messages to most of the crowned heads of the world and to the ecclesiastical heads of all the major religions.

He managed to publish several volumes of his teachings and a commentary on the sacred scriptures of other faiths.

In 1863, he proclaimed himself to be the One whose coming had been foretold by the Bab, namely the Prophet of the Lord who was to usher in his Kingdom of Righteousness and Peace. He was at once enthusiastically accepted as such by the majority of the Bab's followers, who were thereafter known as the Bahais. The Bahais today look upon the Bab as the John the Baptist of their movement, upon Baha'u'llah as their Messiah, and upon his son, Abdul Baha, as their Apostle Paul and greatest missionary.

Abdul Baha visited this country several years ago. It was my privilege to see and hear him at a large gathering in Tremont Temple of Boston during my seminary days. I shall never forget the mental picture which I have of him, a picture of a man of simple dignity and spiritual beauty with a resonant voice that commanded confidence.

The bodies of these three men now rest in tombs on the summit of Mount Carmel in Palestine. Their unity in death, fittingly symbolizes their spiritual unity in life and the oneness of their gospel for all mankind.

What are the chief teachings of their gospel? They can be summarized under twelve points:

1. First of all, this gospel proclaims the oneness of mankind.

"Ye are all the leaves of one tree and the fruits of one orchard," declared Baha'u'llah. There are no chosen peoples, no superior races and no preferred castes. By the same token, there are no infidels, no untouchables and no inferior races. All humanity is equally sacred and precious in the eyes of God.

2. This gospel proclaims the oneness of religion. All faiths — Hindu, Christian, Jewish, Mohammedan, Buddhist and Confucian, are basically the same. Their peculiarities and differences are superficial and due to the accidents of climate, geography and economic conditions. There is one great spiritual reality behind them all. Search out the common denominator of their respective teachings and cling to this as the way of salvation for all the world. Philosophically, all religions agree; it is only in their mythology and ritual that they develop differences.

3. This gospel proclaims the oneness of truth. The truths of science and the truths of religion *cannot* in the *very nature of things contradict each other*. Knowledge of the physical world and knowledge of the spiritual world are not antithetical but complementary. When they seem to arrive at opposite

conclusions, they must correct their theories and begin all over again. Religion must strive to be more reasonable. Science must take more account of spiritual facts.

4. This gospel proclaims the duty of making a fresh and independent investigation of the truth in every generation. No one should blindly follow what his ancestors believed or accept anything on the authority of tradition. Each individual must see with his own eyes, hear with his own ears and think out the truth for himself with his own mind. A statement of the truth may be valid for one age and not valid for another because the meanings of the same words change from one generation to another.

5. Religion, in order to qualify as such, must become a cohesive factor in human society. If your particular form of religion does not bring you into a closer understanding of your fellow men than before you embraced it, then discard it for another form that will. Creeds, dogmas, ceremonies and rituals which make for bigotry, intolerance and fanatical hatred are a denial of real religion.

6. Equality between men and women, politically and socially.

7. The abandonment of all discriminations based on class, cultural, national, racial or religious distinctions.

8. A universal, simultaneous program of disarmament.

9. A universal compulsory program of education.

10. A universal supplementary language to be used as a means of international communication so that eventually all that the future citizen will need to move freely among his fellow men is to learn only two languages, his own mother tongue and the international one.

Keep in mind that Baha'u'llah made this recommendation fully twenty years before Esperanto or any of the other proposed world languages were invented.

11. The spiritual solution of economic problems is stressed. Charity and philanthropy are not enough. Men

cannot claim to be generous until they have first been just. No man should be allowed to live by the toil of others whatever the system of exploitation. All forms of slavery must be abolished, chattel, feudal, and industrial. The economic order must become a partnership, a cooperative affair, and democratic in its management.

Finally, Baha'u'llah proclaimed the necessity of an international court, an international congress, and an international police force, looking forward to the complete abolition of war, and the reign of international law and order under some kind of world federation.

Keep in mind that all these concepts were announced fully eighty years ago in a region which at that time was filled with political intolerance and fanatical bigotry.

Thus far, the followers of Baha'u'llah have been reasonably faithful to his spiritual leadership. The present guardian of the faith, Shoghi Effendi, the great grandson of the founder, is a man of wisdom and high moral stature. The Bahai faith is not only willing but eager to cooperate with every movement, looking to the advancement of the brotherhood of man on earth. It has honestly striven to remain a leavening influence in the world and to avoid becoming merely another religion to divide and confuse the loyalties of mankind.

Of course, many other laudable attempts have been made in the past to search out and emphasize only those truths common to all religions besides the Bahai movement, which sprang from the loins of the Mohammedan faith. The Brahmo Samaj in India had this as its declared objective and continues to do so. The Indian lyric poet, Kabir, tried to find this unity during the Middle Ages. In more recent times, Reformed Judaism, the recent revival of Moism in China, and both the Unitarian and the Universalist churches, have dedicated themselves to the same great concern.

More than a century and a half ago, even before the birth

of Baha'u'llah, Unitarian and Universalist churches had begun reading in their pulpits from the sacred scriptures of
all religions and have been doing so ever since.

We must not overlook the fact that it was a Unitarian
minister, the late Dr. Jenkin Lloyd Jones, who, more than
any other, was responsible for the convening of the World
Parliament of Religions in Chicago at the time of its World
Fair. Unitarians and Universalists took the initiative in
calling the World Congress of Religious Liberals which met
at Amsterdam in the summer of 1949 and which included
delegates from various world religions.

Religious liberals have long recognized the Bahai faith as
kindred to their own in mind and spirit.

If there is any fault to be found with Bahaism, it is that
which we find among religions generally, and this is the
temptation to set up standards of orthodoxy. For example,
we note that the bulk of Bahai publications appear to come
from one family, namely, from Baha'u'llah, his son Abdul
Baha and Abdul's grandson, Shoghi Effendi, the latter using
the designation "Guardian of the Bahai Faith."

Furthermore, as we understand it, Shoghi Effendi was
not elected "Guardian of the Faith" by the members of his
faith, but appointed by his own grandfather. The question
naturally arises, Is not this a dangerous precedent? A seed
that may grow into a tree of orthodoxy and may even put
this faith at the mercy of an hereditary apostolic succession,
which could ultimately defeat the most cherished hopes of
this movement as such successions have always done in the
past?

All liberal religious groups have had to battle constantly
against the temptation to become set and rigid in doctrine
in spite of an oft-declared allegiance to the free mind principle.

All liberals have had to resist repeated attempts to read
certain minority groups out of their particular movement,

the most recent attempt involving the objections of orthodox theists to humanists — thus far with little success.

Bahais must also be on guard against the same temptation, even though it may not seem at first thought to be a real and present danger.

Nevertheless, what Bahais want, liberals desire also, and liberals believe they desire it just as intensely, namely: a world at peace, under a common law and order, united in one brotherhood of the human race; a world mindful of the superficial character of most differences, and of the wisdom of being ready to arbitrate them in the spirit of good will and good faith.

16

Mary Baker Eddy and the Conquest of Fear

The chief stones in the temple of Christian Science are to be found in the following postulates: that Life is God, good, and not evil; that Soul is sinless, not to be found in the body; that Spirit is not, and cannot be, materialized; that Life is not subject to death; that the spiritual real man has no consciousness of material life or death.

Science reveals the glorious possibilities of man, unlimited by the mortal senses. The Christ-element in the Messiah made him the Way shower, Truth and Life.

— MARY BAKER EDDY

WHY SHOULD THE FAITH founded by Mrs. Mary Baker Eddy be classed as one of the world religions instead of merely one of the several denominations of Christianity?

It is because Christian Science represents so pronounced a departure from the orthodox doctrines of the main body of the Christian Church as to amount to a new religion, just as Buddhism, springing from the loins of Hinduism, departed so widely from its spiritual mother that it has long been regarded as a distinct and separate faith.

Mary Baker Eddy, the founder of Christian Science, was one of the three truly remarkable women born in America during the nineteenth century — the other two being Susan

B. Anthony and Helen Keller. The fact that one cannot accept her teachings in full or even in large part should not prevent the recognition of the strength of her character and the enduring worth of much that she achieved.

Millions of people look upon her as the greatest religious genius since the birth of Jesus and accord her a reverence akin to adulation. The star of her spiritual influence, which many critics prophesied would rapidly wane after her death in 1910, has, on the contrary, steadily ascended. Her following was never greater than it is today. Her churches can be found in all the major cities from Maine to California, adorning the most strategic places in these cities and gathering under their imposing domes many of their prominent citizens. Even in the small towns and villages can be found Christian Science reading rooms. Furthermore, the activities of this movement have by no means been confined to this country, but have spread to the far corners of the earth.

When millions of good people leave the faith in which they were reared to embrace another, there must be some important truth in that faith, whatever its limitations. When millions of honest and intelligent people render sincere homage to a certain personality, there must be something of virtue and beauty in that personality worthy of our serious emulation. Such I believe to be the case with Christian Science and its famous founder. You and I as professed seekers after the truth are bound in all sincerity to search for the wheat amidst the chaff which can be found in this as in all religions. It is not enough merely to point out the chaff. It is not the chaff in any religion which sustains the spiritual vitality of its adherents, but its life-giving kernel of truth. And this it is which you and I must learn to distinguish from the chaff.

I can vividly recall the year 1910 when Mrs. Eddy died. I was then attending a divinity school not far from the scene of her lifework. I remember how the newspapers and magazines were filled with controversial articles about her. Some of them were none too complimentary. I can recall some of the disparaging remarks that were made about her life and her faith at that time, some of them taking the form of crude jests and jokes. I confess that the total impression was one to prejudice the average person against her and the faith she founded. During the years following World War I, when the debunking of famous historical personalities was then much in vogue, I remember reading what was alleged to be an objective and realistic biography of Mrs. Eddy, but which I now recognize as a very partial and one-sided picture of the woman and her work.

Mark Twain once wrote an amusing account of Christian Science in which he made ironical sport of the whole movement. But he lived to change his mind and say of Mrs. Eddy, "She has organized and made available a healing principle that for two thousand years has never been employed except as the merest kind of guesswork. She is the benefactor of the age."[1]

Doctor William Mayo of the Mayo Clinic has said, "I have sent people to Christian Scientists and they have got relief."[2]

The distinguished physician, Doctor Richard C. Cabot, recently head of the Massachusetts General Hospital, has said, "Christian Science has done a great deal of good."[3]

Many religious liberals, unable to go the whole way with the Christian Scientists, nevertheless recognize that they are in possession of a profound truth.

The founder of this faith was born in a village just outside of Concord, N. H., July 16, 1821, the daughter of Mark and Abigail Baker and the youngest of six children. Her parents were of good New England stock with a background of religion and culture. They were members of the Congregational Church. Her early childhood was normal and remarkably happy. She enjoyed a close companionship with her oldest brother that approached the ideal.

At twenty-two years of age, she was married to George Washington Glover, who, although a Northerner by birth, was engaged in business at Charleston, South Carolina. The issue of slavery was uppermost in men's minds at that time. Mary Baker was opposed to slavery. Her husband owned slaves and defended the institution. She would have freed them. Within a year, her husband died in an epidemic of yellow fever. She returned to her father's home and later gave birth to the child of this marriage, naming him George Washington Glover, II, in honor of her husband. She endeavored to salvage as much of her husband's estate as possible, but it was not enough to support her and her child. For one thing, she allowed the slaves that were now hers to go free.

She found it difficult to earn a livelihood and finally had to turn over the care of her child to relatives and friends. Her anxiety about his welfare and her own economic plight brought her to a state of semi-invalidism. Hungry for affection and security and hoping to improve her health thereby, she married eight years later a Doctor Daniel Patterson, a well-dressed but rather impractical itinerant dentist, who at first gave her much tenderness and sympathy, but very little in the way of financial support because he had only little to give. Instead of getting better in health, she went from bad to worse. It was her husband, however, who made the arrangements for her to meet Dr. Phineas Quimby of Portland, Maine, who was then enjoying a growing reputation as a hypnotist and physician, able to cure certain diseases where others had failed.

It was not until a full year later that the sick woman was finally able to make the journey to Portland to be treated by Dr. Quimby, but this proved to be the great turning point in her life. Dr. Quimby told her that she was being held in bondage by the opinion of her family and physician, and her animal spirit was reflecting its grief upon her body and calling it spinal disease. After being treated, she testifies that her pain and weakness disappeared at once and a sense of comfort and well-being took their place. Something must have happened because within a week she was able to climb unaided the one hundred and eighty-two steps leading to the dome of the City Hall of Portland. It is true that she later on had relapses but whenever she went to see Dr. Quimby, she was able to recover lost ground.

Not content with her own recovery, she made every attempt to explore the secret behind it. The more she inquired, the more she came to the conclusion that it was her own faith that had actually brought about the transformation and not anything Dr. Quimby had done. She was driven to search the Scriptures more diligently, reviewing the tales of how Jesus and the apostles were able to perform wonders in healing disease without the aid of medicine. She decided that something priceless in the heritage of Christianity had been lost through the centuries, and it was her duty to restore it. She wrote down her thoughts and published them.

The first edition of *Science and Health with Key to the Scriptures* was brought out in the fall of 1875. She was then in her fifty-fifth year. From this point on, she had a mission in life for the first time, to which she devoted the remainder of her days.

She gave every ounce of her energy to spreading the gospel she had found and organizing the Christian Science Church. Everything else was of secondary consideration. Her second husband, Dr. Patterson, had been taken prisoner by the South during the Civil War and the two were long separated and really never got together again. She finally obtained a divorce on grounds of desertion.

Her third marriage to Mr. Asa G. Eddy in 1877, a ceremony performed by a Unitarian minister of Lynn, Massachusetts, proved to be a most happy and fortunate one. He gave her intelligent and sympathetic cooperation until his death five years later. He it was who organized the first Christian Science Sunday school and he was the first to put on to a sign the words: "Christian Science." Until her death in 1910, Mrs. Eddy kept a sacred shrine in her heart for his memory.

She has been called a charlatan and fraud, but no charlatan or fraud could have achieved the enduring good which she has achieved. The general course of her life was in the direction of helping humanity. Her abiding purpose after she made her first discovery was to bring comfort to the brokenhearted, healing to the sick, hearing to the deaf and sight to the blind. She was an earnest and indefatigable searcher after the truth. She wanted to know God at first hand. She showed great strength of character and persistency of purpose which carried her through many a trying situation where others with less courage would have given up in despair and confusion.

She possessed the genius of organization. She was one of the four founders of religion who lived to see their faith become an assured successs, the other three being Zoroaster, Buddha and Mohammed.

Here was a woman, frail in body, a helpless invalid for the greater part of her life, who, by the sheer power of her will and faith, rose to a commanding position of influence in a hostile world. Considering the worst about her, acknowledged by her friends, and the best conceded by her enemies, she was a woman of great spiritual stature.

It is only fair to state that she never once made any special claim to divinity, except as all are stamped with the divine Image. Realizing that she was becoming the object of a growing adulation on the part of her disciples, she saw danger in it and sought to discourage it in these words: "To think or speak of me in any manner as a Christ is sacrilegious." As she approached old age, she more and more tried to turn the attention of her disciples away from her person to her teachings. She firmly discouraged pilgrimages to her home,

She requested that no one should try to communicate with her except through the official board of trustees of the Mother Church in Boston, and she avoided public appearances as much as possible. One might think this was all a clever scheme to enhance her reputation by surrounding it with mystery. On the contrary, there is evidence to support the contention that she was entirely sincere and was anxious to use her strength to improve and clarify her message to the world. Therefore, let us turn from the messenger to the message.

What was the great truth Mrs. Eddy came to bring? It is said to be contained in the book entitled *Science and Health with Key to the Scriptures.* This is the storehouse which contains the precious grain of her harvest. Let us open this storehouse and see what we can find.

I confess for one that I find the vocabulary which Mrs. Eddy uses difficult to understand. I find numerous ordinary words capitalized to give them added significance. I find Biblical expressions given an allegorical interpretation, and familiar terms more or less arbitrarily redefined. In the back of the book she lists about one hundred and twenty-five words and the special sense in which she employs them. Perhaps Mrs. Eddy felt it necessary to create a new vocabulary in order to express what she had to say. I do not find here the same simplicity and lucidity of style which I find, for example, in the Parables and Beatitudes of Jesus as recorded in the Gospels according to Matthew, Mark and Luke. It is more like the language used in the Fourth Gospel of John, where a less concrete and more abstract vocabulary is employed. Nevertheless, if one is willing to study carefully the book as a whole, one's patience will be rewarded.

Someone has said that Christian Science is neither Christian nor scientific. In a technical sense this charge is true. The method Mrs. Eddy uses is the exact opposite of the scientific. Science does not begin with a theory, however plausible, but begins with the facts of life, however obstinate and then tries to arrive by induction at a theory to explain them. Mrs. Eddy, on the other hand, does begin with a theory about God and the universe and attempts to make the facts of life fit into her theory and rejects the facts which do not fit in as mere illusions of the mortal mind. In other words, here is the speculative and deductive method of arriving at the truth, which is the exact opposite of the method commonly called the scientific. And yet, Mrs. Eddy was scientific in appealing to certain facts of life which too many scientists had hitherto unscientifically ignored. As Jesus of Nazareth said, "If any man will do his will, he shall know of the doctrine," so she urged her followers to "demonstrate the truth of Christian Science."

The Christianity of Christian Science is nearer to the Christianity of the third century Gnostics (which was declared a heresy by the main body of the early Christian Church) than it is to what has been recognized as historical Christian doctrine. The Gnostics argued that it did not make any difference whether Jesus as a physical being ever lived or not. They were interested in the spiritual Christ — the Eternal Word who was from the beginning. Furthermore, if one makes a distinction between the Christianity of Jesus as recorded in the Synoptic Gospels and that as recorded in the Gospel of John, it is the latter Christian Science resembles more than the former. As a matter of fact, Mrs. Eddy's basic concept that the real world is a perfect creation and that pain, death, the evil of the natural, material world are illusions of mortal mind, can be traced back to the philosophy of Bishop Berkeley, then to the third century Gnostics, then to Plato's philosophy — and, perhaps, finally, to the ideas of the Brahmans of India.

To say this, however, is not to disparage the unique contribution of Mrs. Eddy. She did not claim to be original. On the contrary, she claimed to be restoring something that once was vital in the religious experience of the early Christians, namely, their power to heal the sick, alleviate pain and conquer fear. By the sheer audacity of her imagination, she has brought the Western world to re-examine the claims of a wholesome, positive psychology toward life in general and especially the power of the mind over the material body. She has called our attention to the fact that many of the aches and ills of mankind are due directly to an unhealthy state of the imagination and the emotions, to fear and worry, to hatred and thoughts of revenge, and that by turning one's thoughts into the positive channels of hope and love and faith and cheerfulness, physical health as well as spiritual vitality will follow.

The conquest of foolish and excessive fears: fear of ourselves, fear of other people, fear of disease, accident, old age and death — the conquest of such fears by the adoption of a positive and radiant faith, this is one of the great contributions of Mary Baker Eddy.

Furthermore, we owe to her a much-needed emphasis on the philosophy of idealism. In an age suffering from an obsession with materialistic gains and materialistic standards, she has inspired millions to find higher spiritual goals and serve more enduring values. Hers has been a mighty protest against the crass and blatant sensualism of our day.

She has given us the example of an efficient church that worships not only one day a week, but every day. She has brought the daily reading of the Bible and the practice of prayer and meditation back into the life of many homes which had long neglected them. She has rebuked the feverish hurry of our modern age which can find time for everything under the sun except the cultivation of inward peace and composure.

The loyalty of Christian Scientists to their faith should put to shame all whose worship is merely a matter of convenience or respectability.

In the fourth place, Mrs. Eddy has set before us the example of a wholesome newspaper by the establishing of *The Christian Science Monitor,* a daily which features the positive, the noble, and the important in current events, rather than crime, scandal and ephemeral gossip, and the sensational. Mrs. Eddy, who chose the name for this daily paper, laid down its general policy and rallied behind it the full backing of the church she had founded. With no journalistic experience, and against the warnings even of friends that such a venture could not succeed financially, she took full responsibility for launching what has since become one of the most widely read and most successful daily newspapers in the world.

Finally, we owe to Mrs. Eddy the emancipation of thousands, if not millions, from the clutches of a crippling orthodoxy. She dared to think for herself, even though she had to break with the creeds and dogmas in which she had been reared. She has played a liberalizing role, by inspiring others to think for themselves as they never dared before. For, in making the leap from the crag of orthodox Christianity to the position of Christian Science, many have fallen in between and, after picking themselves up and dusting off their intellectual garments, have gone forth to explore the whole mountain of truth, as represented by the study of comparative religion. Some of these have become religious liberals, and some even ministers of liberal religion. For these reasons alone, if for no others, we too are grateful for the life of Mary Baker Eddy and join with our Christian Science brethren in blessing her memory.

We do not like the overcentralized character of the organization which she has set up. It permits no democratic control over church policies and principles. Decisions are handed down from above. Democracy in America and elsewhere can best be supported by the practice of democracy on the part of all churches.

Furthermore, we cannot believe that the truth Mrs. Eddy

proclaimed is the whole truth about life and religion. When
she stresses the supremacy of the spiritual over the physical,
the influence of the mind over the body, we find ourselves in
full agreement with her. But the facts of life indicate that
this influence is not a one-way street but moves in both directions. In other words, we believe that the body also influences
the mind. The poet, Robert Browning, has expressed our
attitude thus:

"All good things
Are ours, nor soul helps flesh more, now, than flesh helps soul!"

Yes, soul helps flesh and flesh helps soul. Mrs. Eddy, by
rescuing the first half of this truth from its long neglect by a
materialistic age, bringing it back once more into the foreground of religious concern, has rendered an invaluable
service to all mankind. This is her major contribution and
her enduring worth. And, for this, we cannot be too grateful.

Christian Scientists and religious liberals cannot be too
far apart in their real worship, for the Christian Science
hymnal and one of the recent hymnals of the liberal faith,
Hymns of the Spirit, contain something like a hundred hymns
in-common. When men ascend the mount of highest aspira-
tion they are inevitably brought closer one to another.

17

Karl Marx and the Religion of Communism

From each according to his abilities, to each according to his needs.

— KARL MARX

Eleanor further told me also that her father [Karl Marx] hardly ever spoke about religion; neither for nor against. Her mother and elder sister attended sometimes Mr. Bradlaugh's Sunday services, but father dissuaded them from doing so. He had a dislike of secularism. He told mother that if she wanted edification or satisfaction of her metaphysical needs she would find them in the Jewish prophets rather than in Mr. Bradlaugh's shallow reasonings.

— MAX BEER

THE MOST PERILOUS CLEAVAGE among men today exists not between the so-called capitalist and noncapitalist worlds but between the Communist and noncommunist. For in the present struggle between East and West, most of the Socialist and semi-Socialist governments are making common cause with the capitalistic governments for the defense of their common democratic heritage against totalitarianism.

What hope is there of avoiding a cataclysmic clash between these two worlds? However large or little that hope, it could be much larger were both worlds to understand some of the religious aspects of Communism and govern themselves accordingly. That is to say, both worlds must realize that if Communism is a religion, it can neither be successfully advanced nor successfully combatted in the end by the use of force.

Recently Arnold J. Toynbee said: "For the first time for more than 250 years our Western way of life has been challenged by a religion that rejects it, denounces it, and preaches an alternative way of spiritual life . . . communism is an antiwestern religion of western origin. . . ."

Let us not be deceived by the antireligious professions of this movement. Several of the world religions began by denying the truth of all existing religions.

When Communism declares that "religion is the opiate of the people," we take it that it obviously does not mean to include itself. In spite of its vehement denial of being a religion, Communism has all the earmarks of a religion save an easily recognizable theology. It already possesses a collection of authoritative scriptures, a calendar of special days in the year to be celebrated, a ritual of distinctive ceremonies for private and public occasions, and a missionary zeal to convert the rest of the world. Not long ago a Communist declared, "You may hinder our cause or you may help it but you can no more prevent its ultimate triumph than you can prevent the dawning of the morning sun. And why? Because we are in league with reality, we are allied with the forces of evolution." What is this but an indirect way of claiming faith in what others have called the Will of God, the same kind of dynamic faith which was the driving force behind the aggressive religions of Zoroaster and Mohammed when both were in the heyday of their influence and on the march.

It is a mistake to regard Communism as a mere economic and political program. It is a religion on the march. It is not the reputed goals of Communism which constitute the major fear of the non-Communist world today, but rather the aggressive and violent methods Communism employs to attain its goals. Most of the goals Communism seeks are cherished also by the Socialists, but they are as much opposed to Communist tactics as the staunchest champions of free enterprise. The chief difference between Communists and Socialists today lies in the means each would use to reach the ends both share in common. Both seek a planned economy through the public ownership of all means of production and distribution that are publicly necessary. The latter would rely on parliamentary methods and the slower process of education, whereas the former would resort to direct action and force. And yet both Communists and the more extreme Socialists claim to be faithful disciples of the same great leader, namely Karl Marx.

Pictures of Marx not only adorn the Kremlin and the walls of libraries and workers' clubs throughout the Soviet Union and China but they can be found in the council chambers of many a Socialist cabinet minister exercising political authority in Europe today.

The biography and philosophy of Marx are being seriously studied on both sides of the Iron Curtain. An understanding of the times in which we live requires some understanding of the life and teachings of this man.

Karl Marx, like many another champion of the disinherited, came of a highly cultured family. He was born in the city of Treves, Germany, near the Rhine, in the year 1818. Both his father and mother were descended from a long line of Jewish rabbis, but before their son was six years of age these parents had been converted to the Christian faith and it was in the schools of this faith that Marx received his elementary education.

We note that at the age of seventeen, he matriculated at the University of Bonn in order to prepare himself for the profession of the law, his father being a successful jurist. Becoming more interested, however, in philosophy, history, and literature than in law, he decided to enter Berlin University, there to study under the scholars in these various fields of learning. This experience proved to be the major turning point in his life.

It was while he was attending courses at Berlin University that Marx embraced the Hegelian philosophy. The critical or dialectical methods of Hegel gripped his imagination and led directly to his own later discoveries and postulates in the realm of economics and sociology. How there can be any logical connection between the idealism of Hegel — which holds that the world of things is but the shadow of the world of ideas — and the materialism of Marx, which teaches that the world of ideas is but the shadow of the world of things, is too complicated a story to tell at this point. It is sufficient for our purposes to know that Marx himself again and again acknowledged his debt to Hegel.

At the early age of twenty-three, this brilliant student received the degree of Doctor of Philosophy from Jena University. Ambitious to make the most of his life, he abjured all thoughts of a merely respectable career. This decision caused his father considerable disappointment. No one can read the correspondence between the elder Marx and his son without sensing the tenderness of the father toward the son and the high-mindedness of both.

Possessing already a reputation as a radical and nonconformist, Karl was refused a lectureship at Bonn University which he strongly coveted. Thereupon he turned to freelance journalism. He became the editor of the *Rhenish Gazette,* a liberal newspaper dealing with labor and economic problems. He soon retired, however, from this position to devote more of his time to study. It was during this retirement that he married Jennie von Westphalen, the charming and cultured daughter of a German Privy Counsellor. Probably few of the great men of history ever had a more devoted, loyal and helpful wife than Marx. Aristocratic by inheritance, highly educated, accustomed to luxury and leisure, a brilliant conversationalist, this woman shared without the slightest evidence of complaint the poverty and tribulations which attended the later life of her husband. Marx from this time forth never gave any of his writings to the public without first submitting them to the criticism of his wife.

At the age of twenty-six, he emerged from his retirement and study to declare himself a convinced Socialist. He went to Paris to take up the editorship of the Franco-German Year Books which dealt with the various schools of political economy. Only one number of the Year Book appeared. This book contained among other contributions an article by one Frederick Engels, a young businessman from Manchester, England, who condemned the prevailing economic system in the name of justice but refused to accept the Socialist utopias of Robert Owen and William Morris.

Marx and Engels were immediately attracted to each other, and thus began one of the most loyal and enduring friendships on record — a friendship which made it possible for Marx to continue his literary career, although at times amidst great hardships. Without the help of Engels, Marx with his impractical but proud and uncompromising disposition most probably would have perished in exile.

Possessing uncommon business ability, Frederick Engels was able to follow a career of social radicalism and yet at the same time make enough money to support himself and subsidize his radical friend. These two in 1848 became the joint authors of the now famous *Communist Manifesto,* which constitutes the Torah of today's Socialist and Communist movements. The fundamental proposition which forms the nucleus of this manifesto, namely the theory of the economic interpretation of history, primarily belongs to Marx rather than Engels if we are to credit the expressed declaration of the latter.

Much of the later writings of Marx are nothing more than elaborations of this central doctrine, which Communist and some Socialist scholars believe is destined to do for history what Darwin's theory of the survival of the fittest has done for biology.

Forced to leave Paris at the instigation of the Prussian government, Marx fled to Brussels with all his belongings. There he joined the League of the Just, a Communistic society of German workers which later changed its name to that of "The Communist League."

In 1848, revolution broke out in both France and Germany. Marx took advantage of the situation to return to his native country and re-establish the *Rhenish Gazette*. Fearless and uncompromising, he championed the cause of the revolution. He advocated the nonpayment of taxes and the organization of armed resistance to the King of Prussia. The revolution, however, failed. Marx was arrested and tried for high treason. He was unanimously acquitted but was eventually obliged to flee his native land once more. France proved to be an unfriendly refuge. He was given the option of deportation or isolation in a small French village. He decided to accept deportation and selected London as his future place of residence.

It is in London that he found opportunity to complete his studies in economics and history. He made almost daily trips to the British Museum. It is here that he wrote his monumental work, *Das Kapital,* which has been called the Bible of the working class.

It is here that Marx suffered the greatest hardships of his life, being compelled by dire financial straits to occupy a few small dingy rooms in the slum district of the city. On one occasion he pawned his last coat in order to get money to publish his books.

It is here that he founded the First International Working Men's Association. It is here that he wrote his famous articles for the *New York Tribune* in support of the Northern side of the Civil War. It is here that he remained for the rest of his life except for short excursions to continental health resorts. It was in London that he died in 1883 at the age of sixty-five, just a few months after the death of his devoted wife.

The three most significant doctrines of Marx, the theories of surplus value, the class struggle, and the economic interpretation of history, are still a matter of dispute in intellectual circles. The fundamental hypothesis of Darwin has been widely accepted by scientific scholarship throughout the world, but the Marxian propositions have not been so accepted. The disciples of Marx claim that the immediate economic interests of the world's scholarship are jeopardized by these propositions, and the refusal to recognize them is but one more proof of their validity!

Whether the Marxian doctrines are eventually widely accepted or rejected, no one who is informed can deny their present incalculable service to mankind by directing attention to the grave injustices and inequities of our prevailing social order. No one can deny that his vision of a commonwealth of man has brought to the hapless victims of unemployment and poverty throughout the earth a large measure of hope for a better day to come. No one can deny that his criticisms constitute the severest challenge to our existing laws and institutions.

The body of Karl Marx lies buried in Highgate Cemetery in London, but his mind and imagination still confront mankind. He is more alive today than ever before.

Professed atheist and materialist, scorner of all religions though he was, he nevertheless lived his life on a spiritual plane, a life actuated by the highest motives of service to humanity. He chose to minister to the lowly and disinherited of the earth. His own life is a refutation of his materialistic philosophy.

Hater of tyranny, courageous champion of race equality and economic justice, persistent seeker after the truth, whatever may become of his doctrines eventually, the sincerity and consecration of the man himself will be an inspiration to his fellow men for years to come. His dream of a classless society and a peaceful and highly productive world, ruled by the principle "From each according to his ability, to each according to his need," is certainly not inconsistent with the highest ideals of religion, however much the methods of his followers have betrayed these ideals.

The peril of his challenge to our day does not lie in whatever truth he discovered but rather in the arrogant assumption of a large group of his followers that his is the whole truth. It is this very assumption that any truth is the whole truth that constitutes one of the real devils which have regularly appeared and reappeared down through the centuries to play havoc with man's most cherished aspirations for a happy and peaceful social order. It is a devil that must be resisted, whether incarnated in the form of a totalitarian state, totalitarian party, or a totalitarian church, but in resisting it we must beware of the temptation to take on the characteristics of the very evil we would resist.

The immediately most perilous cleavage among men today is undoubtedly between the Communist and non-Communist worlds, but the wider and more difficult breach to heal is still that which exists between the liberal world on the one hand and the authoritarian world on the other, whether of the Right or the Left. It can be healed only by a return to democratic ideals on the part of authoritarians, for there can be no middle ground between lovers of liberty and lovers of tyranny. In the face of the tensions of our world, democracy must assert itself against totalitarianisms of the Right and of the Left whose methods imply the destruction of our liberties.

18

Gandhi and the Power of Soul Force

It was the New Testament which really awakened me to the rightness and value of Passive Resistance. When I read in the "Sermon of the Mount" such passages as "Resist not him that is evil but whosoever smiteth thee on thy right cheek turn to him the other also," and "Love your enemies and pray for them that persecute you, that ye may be sons of your Father which is in heaven," I was simply overjoyed, and found my own opinion confirmed where I least expected it. *The Bhagavad Gita* deepened the impression, and Tolstoi's "The Kingdom of God is Within You" gave it permanent form.

— GANDHI

ONE OF THE MOST MOMENTOUS EVENTS of our time and of all time took place when India and Pakistan recently became independent and self-governing dominions.

Thus has ended in partial victory at least one of the longest and certainly one of the most amazing struggles in the annals of human freedom. And the chief credit for this victory goes by common consent to an emaciated aged man who never once wielded any weapon except the sword of the spirit.

Let us acknowledge the fact that the example of the United States of America in giving independence to the Philippines may have contributed to Britain's withdrawal from India. Let us give much credit to the statesmanship of the British government and to the natural decency and sense of fair play of the British people. Let us make due allowance for the fact that Britain's economic plight made it necessary for her to curtail her ambitions of empire in other cases as well as in India. Let us recognize the superb statesmanship of Pandit Nehru and the enormous role he has played.

But, after all is said and done, the great achievement of a free India is pretty much a monument to the intelligence and driving force of one man, Mohandas K. Gandhi, better known as Mahatma Gandhi. This man, in the midst of a world up to its knees in blood and violence, vindicated the power of idealism, of nonviolence and of soul force — on a colossal scale. With his humanitarian heart, his dynamic will and his realistic mind, he is to many the most outstanding personality of this age. Winston Churchill, Joseph Stalin, Chiang Kai-shek, Adolf Hitler, and Franklin Delano Roosevelt have loomed large on the horizon of our times. But when the perspective of several generations has come, it is not improbable that all these will seem small in comparison with the towering spirit of this frail Hindu statesman.

"A man like Gandhi," says Bernard Shaw, "comes only once in a thousand years."

Yes, India has achieved freedom. But what about the bloodshed that is sporadically taking place in that unhappy land? What about the strife between Moslem and Hindu and the wholesale rioting and destruction of property which have come as the aftermath of independence? It is true that a complete victory has not yet been won. For peace as well as independence has been all along one of the higher goals of Gandhi's heroic struggles. But, in the midst of whatever violence and strife there is, can still be heard his calm and courageous voice once more, pleading for sanity and reconciliation. With freedom gained, he plunged into the most difficult and the most important undertaking of his active career, viz., the healing of Hindu and Moslem differences.

And how great those differences must be! What have Hindu and Moslem in common? Arab and Jew seem to believe that they have a difficult time understanding each other. But both claim spiritual descent from Abraham, and both have in common the inspiring and commanding personality of Moses. Christian and Jew think they have little basis for understanding each other, but both have in common not only Abraham and Moses, but also the great prophets Amos, Hosea, Isaiah, and Jeremiah, and even a common book of hymns and prayers in the Psalms. Protestant and Catholic do not find it easy to comprehend each other's point of view, and yet, they have even more in common. They have both the Old Testament and the New Testament. They have Jesus of Nazareth, Saul of Tarsus, as well as Abraham, Moses and the prophets, and, in addition, many ceremonies and liturgies and what should not be overlooked — a large common religious vocabulary.

But what have the Moslems and Hindus as a basis for understanding? Very little indeed: there are no scriptures which they share together; no heroes, no prophets, no customs and no religious vocabulary to hold them together; nothing but the Golden Rule and a common respect for the spiritual grandeur of Mahatma Gandhi, who, because of his sustained use of this one principle, is well on his way to becoming the first hero to be claimed by both Moslem and Hindu alike. While others celebrated the independence of India in riotous jubilation, this man, whom the crowds wanted to carry on their shoulders in triumphant procession as the hero of the hour, was saddened by the renewed outburst of religious strife which followed the celebration.

He went directly to the scenes of greatest violence, there to proclaim a fast unto death in order to shame the bloodthirsty rioters into sanity and repentance. First to Calcutta's restless slums he betook himself; then to Delhi, the capital of Hindu India and the center of savage rioting, there to interpose his spiritual power, to stay the violence of both Hindu and Moslem alike.

"This is not a time for celebration," he cried. "This is a time for silence and prayer. A tooth for a tooth is no remedy. Love is the only lasting cure of hatred." What a sublime truth!

He was cut down by an assassin's bullet as he was going to his accustomed place to pray for the unity of Hindu and Moslem. He was seen to make a gesture in forgiveness of the assassin, just before he himself crumpled to the earth.

Gandhi is dead, but his spirit lives. We believe that his spirit will yet achieve the full victory he had originally in mind, namely, the unity of India as well as its independence. At this distance, living as we do in the midst of a comparatively well-fed people, we can scarcely understand the spiritual appeal of the hunger-strike as employed by him. Among a people who are frequently confronted with real hunger, however, the spectacle of a man whose abilities could command luxurious living and whose motives were above reproach or even suspicion — the spectacle of such a man deliberately imposing hardships on himself because of the sins of other people — did somehow make a tremendous moral appeal, penetrating to the very heart of the most hardened and vicious-minded. Yes, I believe we can count on ultimate victory for Gandhi.

What power of patience and perseverance he possessed! What courage, what spiritual integrity and endurance! How did this man happen to become what he was and still is?

Graduating from the Law School of London University at the age of twenty-three, and having been admitted to the British Bar, Gandhi returned to his native land to practice his profession in which he rapidly rose to a commanding position. It was while on legal business in British South Africa in behalf of one of his clients, that his life was radically changed from a career of private ambition to one of public service. Observing the outrageous conditions of the Indian coolies who were brought to Africa for purposes of exploitation, Gandhi gave up his profession and all his property — which was considerable — to champion and defend his down-trodden fellow-countrymen, living as serfs in a foreign land.

For twenty years he fought a nonviolent battle against the British government, and in the end won a striking vindication, for the political rights which he secured for his people in British South Africa are still in force today.

He obtained his idea of nonviolence from reading the Bhagavad-Gita, but the idea was clarified and greatly re-enforced by studying the works of Leo Tolstoy and Henry Thoreau, particularly the former's famous book entitled, *The Kingdom of God Is Within You*. In 1913, he returned to his own country from British South Africa to lay plans for the emancipation of his people at home.

The story of India in recent years is largely the story of this one man's defiance of an empire. He came to the conclusion that the best way to independence for his people was to inspire them to be worthy of independence. Ignorance, hatred, violence, racial and religious intolerance, he discerned, were the great obstacles in the way. He, himself, would set an example of love, good will, rational behavior and simple, unselfish living.

The first thing he did was to renounce all luxury. He girded himself with a loin cloth, the garb of the lowliest millions. He devised for himself a cheap, but life-sustaining diet of dates and goat milk, and selected only the most necessary furnishings for his home. The next thing he did was to take into his home an outcast girl, one of India's so-called Untouchables. In doing so he defied the tradition of many centuries which had sanctified this wrong, which denied the most elementary rights of humanity to fifty-five million of innocent, helpless men, women and children. No one knows anything about the story of man's inhumanity to man until he becomes acquainted with the story of India's Untouchables, who have long suffered horrible privations and unmentionable humiliations. Wherever Gandhi went, he pleaded the cause of the oppressed people and literally inspired millions to follow his example. Substantial progress has been made within the last ten years. Doctor E. Stanley Jones, one of the authorities on India today, told us that the backbone of the caste system has been broken for good. The rest is a mopping-up process which will naturally take several more years.[1]

The next obstacle Gandhi attacked was religious hatred between Moslem and Hindu, and this he regarded as the most difficult task of all because there are always demagogues in nearly every country ready to exploit hatred for their own ulterior ends. It was a deep-rooted hatred, the product of a vicious circle of fear, superstition and outright persecution which he confronted. But, nothing daunted, Gandhi valiantly made one assault after another on the prejudices, dogmas and superstitions that kept these two great groups of people apart. His strategy was the heroic one of appealing to the divine in man, to man's better nature — a strategy demanding the utmost in patience and skill. He had hoped to achieve both unity and freedom for his country during his lifetime, but he was enough of a realist to accept half of a loaf, rather than none — namely a free India — while he continued his efforts to obtain the other half, a united India as well.

In pursuing these goals, he became the greatest saint of our time, no mean achievement in itself. Saintliness is not a fixed and rigid standard. It is measured in terms of sincerity and effort. The degree to which one lives up to the highest ideals is the measure of one's moral stature. By this test, Gandhi was one of the saintliest of all the saints, and he, while yet living, was revered as such by more people than was any saint in history.

There is nothing which he advocated that he did not first practice in his own life. He so disciplined his appetites and emotions that he became the absolute master of himself. And all this was done, not as an end in itself, but as a means of serving his fellow men.

He would not deviate from the truth by a hair's breadth. For instance, he would not use spies or detectives to find out what his opponents were planning because it involved deception and dishonesy. He would not flinch from what he conceived to be his duty even though it meant long-drawn-out suffering and the hazard of death. He would not allow anyone to become an enemy to be hated under any circumstances whatsoever.

He did nothing for the sake of ostentation or popular applause. His language was simple, direct and free from exaggeration. He denied himself even the luxury of sarcastic speech. In addressing large crowds — and he probably spoke to larger gatherings of people than any man in history — he never raised his voice, but always spoke in calm and even tones.

Every day, he spent several hours at his spinning wheel, by which he partly earned his simple livelihood and which he took with him wherever he went. A symbol of that spinning wheel has become the banner of the new state of India.

Has the picture been overdrawn? Did not this man have any weaknesses and frailties? Yes, of course, but they were largely of the body, not of the mind and heart and will.

With what religious geniuses can we compare him? Can we compare him with Moses? Yes, like Moses, this leader accepted full responsibility for the sins of his followers and did penance in their stead. But, unlike Moses, no blood was shed by his own hands.

Can we compare him with Socrates? Yes, like that brave

Grecian, he went in and out among his fellow men with no fear of death. But, unlike him, he achieved domestic peace and harmony.

Can we compare him with Ignatius Loyola? Yes, like the founder of the Jesuits, Gandhi sought out the lepers and cared for them with his own hands. He did it again and again. But, unlike Loyola, he never acted on the erroneous principle that the end justifies the means. "Better," he said, "to fail of independence than to obtain it by way of physical force."

Can we compare him with Francis of Assisi? Yes, like him, Gandhi was a friend not only of the poor and oppressed but also of birds and beasts as well. But, unlike Francis, he rose far above the narrow dogmas and crude superstitions of the religion into which he was born. The religion of Gandhi can stand the scrutiny of the scientific method.

With whom, then, can we adequately compare him? There is no one except the saintly prophet and founder of the Christian faith, Jesus of Nazareth, who went about doing good, who had compassion on the multitudes, who was a friend of publican and sinners, who said, "Come unto me all ye that labor and are heavy laden, and I will give you rest," who pleaded, "Love your enemies, do good to them which hate you, bless them that curse you, pray for them which despitefully use you. And unto him that smiteth thee on the one cheek offer also the other." In the spirit of those last words was the prayer: "Father, forgive them for they know not what they do." The magic power of love, the spiritual power of good will and nonviolent resistance to evil — this is the heart of Christ's Sermon on the Mount. And this, the essential principle of Christianity, a Hindu vindicated on a scale never before witnessed since the days of Jesus.

Gandhi's faith in the spiritual power of love and good will is the crying need of the hour.

O that he had a seat in the council chambers of the

United Nations! How much the whole world needs his saving sense of sanity and realism.

> Above the strident tumult of the mart
> Where raucous tradesmen barter souls for gain,
> And shamelessly play out a shameful part,
> Thy quiet challenge strikes us to the heart.
> Transcendent faith and love alone remain
> Decisive answers to the base and vain
> Pretensions of the tyrant's evil art,
> All alien rulers waver in dismay
> As carnal weapons prove of no avail.
> Thy nation's bitter sorrow and travail
> Shall win for all mankind a happier day
> When violent men and deeds are swept away
> And the soul's majesty and truth prevail.[2]

19

The Golden Rule in All Religions

> To those who are good to me, I am good; and to
> those who are not good to me, I am also good. And
> thus all get to be good.
> To those who are sincere with me, I am sincere;
> and with those who are not sincere with me, I am also
> sincere. And thus all get to be sincere.
> — Taoist Scriptures

Is THERE ANY REAL HOPE of building a just and lasting peace
among the nations of the world, or are the differences between the various races of mankind so great that such a goal is
utterly fantastic?

Surely it is not unreasonable to hold that a peace based
on force alone cannot long endure.

There must be in addition a widespread will to maintain
peace and sincere cooperation.

All the peoples of the world must learn to understand one
another far better than they have in the past.

Individuals cannot cooperate successfully with one another without first reaching some common basis of mutual
understanding, and this is just as true of nations as of individuals.

If world law and order is ever to be a reality, it means that
Americans, Russians, Chinese, Japanese, Britons, Hindus,
Koreans, Arabs, Jews, Africans, Germans, Italians and all the
others will have to find some common denominator of values

which is shared alike. It cannot be established except upon a foundation of ethical and spiritual agreements.

The present barrier of different languages can be surmounted because we can always resort to interpreters; but if, after we have translated our codes and laws, they still mean one thing to the Russians and Koreans, and something quite different to Britons and Americans, then the project of building a world order will have to be given up, for the very same reason that the Tower of Babel had to be abandoned when the masons and carpenters failed to understand one another A confusion of values is far more of an obstacle to successful cooperation than even a confusion of tongues.

Fortunately, it seems there does exist a basis for world understanding and cooperation. It lies in the fact that the various races of mankind have made an independent discovery of the Golden Rule, either in its positive or negative form. This is a most hopeful sign.

It is just as hopeful a sign as the fact that the chemical composition of human blood is essentially the same in all races. We know now there are four types of blood listed as: O, A, B, and AB, but all of these four types can be found in all races.

Just so there are many superficial differences in the ethical and religious codes of mankind — but one moral standard is common to them all, namely, the Golden Rule.

Christianity says, "All things whatsoever ye would that men should do to you, do ye even so to them."

But a thousand years before Christianity was founded, the Hindu Scriptures said, "The true rule in life is to guard and do by the things of others as you do by your own."[1] Observe the words "guard" and "do."

If all the world were to guard and do by the things of others as though they were their own, we could find the basis for a durable peace at least between the Hindu and Christian world.

Now, let us take the Buddhist faith which came into existence fully five centuries before the Christian era. What does it have to say on this question of man's relation to his fellow man? It lays down essentially the same principle: "One should seek for others the happiness one derives for oneself." Here again, the Golden Rule is expressed in positive form. There are, roughly speaking, three hundred and fifty million Buddhists in the world. If these millions were to live up to this fundamental insight of their own faith, if they were to seek for others the happiness they desire for themselves, we should not need to be disturbed about the security of world peace. In all fairness to the Buddhists, it must be said that there is actually less need to be concerned about them than any other group of people on the face of the earth. For a period of two thousand and five hundred years, the Buddhist faith has inspired only one religious war, and that was a minor affair occurring two thousand years ago in the country of Tibet. The Buddhists are an order-loving people and can be counted on to understand what is required to maintain the peace of the world.

And then, there are the Zoroastrians, at present reduced to a mere hundred thousand in Persia and northwestern India. But this faith also discovered the Golden Rule.

"Do as you would be done by," says the Zend-Avesta, the sacred scriptures of Zoroaster. Here we have not only the same concept, but almost the same words as Jesus used, in shorter form.

We do not know exactly when Zoroaster lived, but his religion was in full force when the Persians captured Babylon and released the Jews who had been taken captive to return to Jerusalem to rebuild the temple there. This event took place in the year 539 B.C.

Zoroastrianism was once one of the chief religions of the Graeco-Roman World. In the days of Jesus it was called Mithraism and constituted the faith of the overwhelming majority of the people from the Straits of Gibraltar to the borders of India. It had considerable influence on the development of Christianity. Mithraism might very well have been responsible for introducing the Golden Rule in its positive form to the Founder of Christianity, although there is no direct evidence to substantiate such a connection.

Judaism, of course, possessed the Golden Rule in its negative form. It was first voiced by Rabbi Hillel who was born about the year 70 B.C. A stranger once came to visit the celebrated rabbi and, wishing to scoff at religion for its many rules, challenged Hillel to teach him the whole of Judaism whilst he stood on one foot. Hillel was ever patient, and never rejected anyone regardless of how impertinent his request seemed to be. He would try to turn his impertinence to profitable account. On this occasion, we are told that the distinguished rabbi was equal to the situation and replied, "What is displeasing to thyself, do not do to others. This is the substance of the law. All else is commentary. Go now and put thy knowledge into practice."

The famous sage, Confucius, gave essentially the same answer, when he, about four centuries earlier, was asked the same question under similar circumstances. Someone wanted to know what he considered to be the true path of life, and Confucius replied, "When one cultivates to the utmost the principles of his own nature and exercises them on the principle of reciprocity, he is not far from the path. What you do not want done to yourself, do not do to others."[2]

There are four hundred million Confucians in the world, and there is perhaps not one in ten who has not at some time or other in his life been taught to memorize and consider the meaning of this saying of Confucius, because it is among the first of his teachings to be stressed. Indeed, much of what he wrote was merely a detailed application of this principle. The tendency of Confucianism has always been to make for law and order. The breaking of the pledged word, the waging of aggressive war, the plundering of other people have never been countenanced by this religion. If all the people of the world were Confucian, the success of international law and order would be almost guaranteed.

Finally, let us turn to the Mohammedans and see what they possess. Yes, they, too, possess the Golden Rule, but in the negative form. "Let none of you treat your brother in a way he himself would dislike to be treated," says the Koran.

There are almost two hundred million Moslems scattered over all the continents except South America and Australia. There are twenty thousand in the United States, five million in Europe, one hundred sixty million in Asia, and forty-five million in Africa. Granted that the Moslems have not lived up to their Golden Rule, it is just as true to state that six hundred million Christians have not lived up to theirs.

The Christian and the Moslem nations have probably had a worse record for upsetting the peace of the world than all the others combined. The Christian's Golden Rule in positive form cannot be said to be superior to the Moslem's in negative form if we are to judge by the international conduct of the Christian as over against the Moslem nations. Nevertheless, they do possess a common ethical insight which can become the basis of mutual understanding and cooperation, and this is equally true of the other peoples of the earth. In short, nine-tenths of the world is more or less already familiar with the same ideal of justice and fair dealing and this is most fortunate indeed.

In this fact alone it seems that we have a real foundation on which to build a more co-operative international society. The Chinese, the Russians, the people of India, Korea, Great Britain and America, as well as the people of other countries, do not need to be angels or saints to make world order a reality.

We in this country know how far short we have come from living up to our own Golden Rule, but as we have learned to reach an understanding sufficient to outlaw war between our several states, it does not seem vain to hope that a reasonable agreement can yet be reached among the various nations to make another such war as the last one wholly unnecessary and impossible, at least for a long time to come. The God who is the Father of us all, has not left any of his children without the spiritual capacity to discern between good and evil, between right and wrong. In the words of the poet, Edwin Markham:

> We men of Earth have here the stuff
> Of Paradise — we have enough!
> We need no other stones to build
> The Temple of the Unfulfilled —
> No other ivory for the doors —
> No other marble for the floors —
> No other cedar for the beam
> And dome of man's immortal dream.
>
> Here on the paths of every-day —
> Here on the common human way
> Is all the stuff the gods would take
> To build a Heaven, to mold and make
> New Edens. Ours the stuff sublime
> To build Eternity in time! [3]

Surely there is enough to build at least an enduring and endurable world order.

20

The Hope Immortal in All Religions

Let us reflect in another way, and we shall see that there is great reason to hope that death is a good; for one of two things — either death is a state of nothingness and utter unconsciousness, or, as men say, there is a change and migration of the soul from this world to another. Now if you suppose that there is no consciousness, but a sleep like the sleep of him who is undisturbed even by dreams, death will be an unspeakable gain. . . . Now if death be of such a nature, I say that to die is gain; for eternity is then only a single night. But if death is the journey to another place, and there, as men say, all the dead abide, what good, O my friends and judges, can be greater than this? . . . Wherefore, O judges, be of good cheer about death, and know of a certainty, that no evil can happen to a good man, either in life or after death. The hour of departure has arrived, and we go our ways — I to die, and you to live. Which is better God only knows.

— SOCRATES

IF A MAN DIE shall he live again? This question, posed by the author of the Book of Job, has intrigued the imagination of all races of men from earliest times down to the present hour. It will undoubtedly continue to do so for countless centuries to come.

186

Let us examine the major historic answers which have been given to this important question by six different peoples of this earth. First, we shall consider the answer of ancient Israel; then, in turn, the answers of ancient Egypt, ancient Persia, classical Greece and Rome, ancient India and the China of Confucius.

While it is undoubtedly true that to some people the thought of life everlasting is an appalling prospect, one to be dreaded rather than desired, we are certainly safe in saying that the vast majority of mankind has a deep-seated longing for some kind of immortality. So keen, so wistful, is this desire to live on indefinitely that many people comfort themselves with the prospect that, come what may, they will continue to live on at least in the lives of their children and their children's children.

The hope of immortality by way of one's descendants was the most substantial immortality that the people of ancient Israel were able to entertain in the period before the Babylonian Exile. The promise made to Abraham that his seed would become as numerous as the sands of the sea and as the stars in heaven enabled them to face death with tranquility and hope.

This is why the lot of the barren woman and the childless man in ancient Israel was regarded as a calamity. For thereby, the magic link of life was broken.

Since there was always the possibility of one's progeny completely dying out sooner or later, there remained only one other prospect of achieving immortality, namely, through the work of one's hands. This is why the author of the Ninetieth Psalm, believing that God had ordained man to return to the dust whence he had come, cried out to heaven for some kind of survival after death when he prayed:

> And let the beauty of the Lord our God be upon us;
> And establish thou the work of our hands upon us;
> Yea, the work of our hands establish thou it.

He could not seriously entertain the hope of his own personal survival, but he found comfort in the faith that at any rate something of what he had been and achieved would abide indefinitely.

The prospect of continuing to live on in the life of our children and in the work of our hands is surely a very real and satisfying kind of immortality and constitutes one of the major motivations of our common human nature. But most people throughout the ages have desired something more. They have cherished the hope of preserving their own identity in a world beyond the grave.

How did this idea that there might be another life enter the mind of man? Perhaps through the experience of dreams. It was noted early in primitive times that when loved ones died they could be seen fully alive in one's dreams. Sometimes even when one was fully awake they appeared as apparitions. With the passing of months and years, these visions of the dead became less frequent and often, sooner or later, ceased altogether. The thought occurred the dead must be still alive. They must still be somewhere or they would not be treading "the dream-led paths of sleep." But why do some seem to make more vivid and lasting impressions in one's dreams than others? Could there possibly be any relation between their life after death and the condition of their mortal remains?

Several ancient peoples came to the conclusion that there was a very important relation. They decided that the afterlife for any given individual was largely if not wholly dependent upon the preservation of his physical body. No one could hope to survive in the world to come, they concluded, unless his corpse remained intact upon earth. Hence the practice of embalming began and the building up of imposing mausoleums.

A vast importance was attached to the interment of the human body. Every energy was bent to keep it from disintegrating after death lest the spirit of the departed would simultaneously disintegrate in the life beyond the grave. This idea spread rapidly throughout the ancient world, or it could have occurred to many different groups of people independently.

At any rate, at the dawn of History we find the idea dominating the thought of one of the greatest civilizations of antiquity, the Egyptian. There the art of mummification reached a high degree of perfection. The energies of the people from king to peasant were focussed upon preserving the mortal remains of their dead. They built gigantic tombs, the Pyramids, as enduring sepulchers, and furnished them lavishly with gold and silver, with beautiful glass and pottery and all kinds of weapons and utensils whose spiritual counterparts they thought might be necessary for the continuance of a satisfactory life in the after world.

Over the inner portal of one of the Egyptian pyramids, built about the year 2000 B.C., we find the following inscription:

These have found grace in the eyes of the Great God. They dwell in the abodes of glory, where the heavenly life is led. The bodies which they have abandoned will repose forever in their tombs, while they will enjoy the presence of the Great God.[1]

There has been a substantial survival of Egyptian funeral customs to our own day, even in this country, which reveals the amazing persistence of this concept of immortality. This concept also prevailed to a large extent among the Indians of both North and South America before the white man came.

When Zoroaster appeared upon the scene in Persia, he deliberately challenged the view that the afterlife was contingent upon the preservation of the human body. Instead of trying to prevent or delay the disintegration of the body after death, he thought it desirable to expedite the process and advocated exposure to the elements on mountain tops and other high places. He proclaimed that there was no need to be disturbed about what happened to the physical remains after death. Since the Creator had once created the whole universe as well as the human body out of nothing, he declared that it would not be much of an additional task for Him to reassemble the original physical frame of every man, woman, and child, whenever it pleased Him. And this He will do on that great day when He will come to judge all the children of men and separate the righteous from the unrighteous — when the righteous shall be transported to Heaven and eternal bliss while the unrighteous shall be condemned to Hell and eternal punishment.

Zoroaster inquired of Ahura Mazda, "Whence does a body form again, which the wind has carried and the water conveyed? and how does the resurrection occur?"

And his God replied:

Observe that when that which was not was then produced why is it not possible to produce again that which was? for at that time one will demand the bone from the spirit of earth, the blood from the water, the hair from the plants, and the life from fire, since they were delivered to them in the original creation.[2]

This concept of immortality through the resurrection of the body on the Day of Judgment was adopted by the Pharisaic wing of Judaism long before the age of Jesus, and later by both Christianity and Islam. It survived in the so-called Apostles' Creed which is reverently repeated in the orthodox Christian churches today. The resurrection of the body is the theme of most Easter music.

Much older than the answer of Zoroaster's Persia is the answer of the priests of Bacchus and Ceres in ancient Rome, and of Dionysus and Demeter in ancient Greece.

If a man die, shall he live again?

Yes, replied the priests of Bacchus and Ceres, provided he partakes of the flesh and blood of Deity and commits no mortal sin between that event and the hour of his death. Man by nature is mortal. Only the gods are immortal. Therefore, if man wants eternal life, he must feed upon the very body of the gods.

But how can this be done? Where can this magic diet be found?

The priests of Bacchus, the wine god, and the priests of Ceres, the goddess of grain, had a specific answer. Wine blessed by the priests of Bacchus was transformed mysteriously into the very blood of the god; and bread, blessed by the priests of Ceres, was just as mysteriously transformed into the very flesh of the goddess. By consuming this wine and this bread, one could be assured of immortality at death, providing one did not commit a mortal offence in the meantime. Since there is always the possibility of committing such an offence before one's death, it is never wise to take any risk in missing an opportunity to partake of the consecrated wine and bread.

This idea, of course, is even much older than the days of Bacchus and Ceres, or of Dionysus and Demeter, their Grecian equivalents. It goes back into remote periods of antiquity when more primitive gods and goddesses required the consumption of the consecrated flesh of animals, and even that of human beings, as the price of eternal life.

Nearly every religion in the world has some remnants of theophagy, which is merely the Greek word for "eating one's God." It is possible to argue that it survives down to our own day in the doctrine of Transubstantiation and in the sacrament of the Holy Eucharist.

Except ye eat the flesh of the Son of man, and drink his blood, ye have no life in you.

Whoso eateth my flesh, and drinketh my blood, hath eternal life; and I will raise him up at the last day.

For my flesh is meat indeed, and my blood is drink indeed.

He that eateth my flesh, and drinketh my blood, dwelleth in me, and I in him.

As the living Father hath sent me, and I live by the Father: so he that eateth me, even he shall live by me.

This is that bread which came down from heaven: not as your fathers did eat manna, and are dead: he that eateth of this bread shall live forever.[3]

Thus within a century after the death of Jesus, his Last Supper with his disciples had been transformed from a simple fellowship meal into a sacrament of immortality.[4] ·

If a man die, shall he live again?

The seers and prophets of ancient India have given an answer to this question entirely different from any we have thus far considered. They proclaimed that the soul of man is indestructible and immortal by its very nature. The human body is only a temporary habitation of this soul. It has had many such habitations and will have many more. Its survival is in no way dependent upon what happens to the physical dwelling places. Man does not achieve eternal life. His life is already eternal.

The Lord Krishna says in the Bhagavad-Gita:

> . . . the wise in heart
> Mourn not for those that live, nor those that die.
> Nor I, nor thou, nor any one of these,
> Ever was not, nor ever will not be,
> For ever and for ever afterwards.
> All, that doth live, lives always! To man's frame
> As there come infancy and youth and age,
> So come there raisings-up and layings-down
> Of other and of other life-abodes,
> Which the wise know, and fear not. . . .

> Never the spirit was born; the spirit shall cease to be never . . .
> Birthless and deathless and changeless remaineth the spirit for
>   ever;
> Death hath not touched it at all, dead though the house of it
>   seems! . . .

> > Nay, but as when one layeth
> > His worn-out robes away,
> > And, taking new ones, sayeth,
> >   "These will I wear to-day!"
> > So putteth by the spirit

> Lightly its garb of flesh,
> And passeth to inherit
> A residence afresh.[5]

This idea of the soul's imperishable and eternal nature was inherited by Buddhism and undergirded its whole philosophy of life.

This is the same concept which we eventually find in such modern philosophers as Immanuel Kant and Ralph Waldo Emerson. Most religious liberals today who confidently believe in immortality base their hope not upon the bodily resurrection of Jesus from the tomb on Easter morn, or upon any other alleged historical event, but upon the argument for the indestructibleness of the human soul, an argument inherited from ancient India by way of Greece and Rome and Palestine.

Whether influenced by Hindu thought or whether he made the discovery independently, the Chinese philosopher Lao-tse also gave expression to the same idea. He frequently referred to the everlasting character of the real life of man. "The man who follows the heavenly way of virtue and wisdom which is the way of the soul," he declared, "is imperishable."

> He who knows the Eternal Law . . . endures for ever.
> Though his body perish, yet he suffers no harm.
>
> Life is a going forth. Death is a returning home. . . .
>
> Man passes through this sublunary life
>   as a white horse passes a crack;
>   here one moment, gone the next!
>
> The bow-sheath is slipped off; the clothes-bag is dropped;
>   and in the confusion the soul wings its flight
>   on the great journey home.[6]

Mo Ti, a young contemporary of Lao-tse, came to the same conclusion. He was confident of the immortality of the soul.

Confucius, however, was not so sure. "We know so little about Life," he said. "How can we speak with confidence about Death?" Confucius disregarded the whole question of immortality as one of those problems beyond the power of man's knowledge to solve, because so little real progress had been made in spite of repeated attempts to solve it. In other words, Confucius was an agnostic in respect to the life after death, and thought it a waste of time to be unduly concerned about it. Let us concentrate on the prolongation and enhancement of the life we know — this seems to have been his general point of view. And this is the reasonable attitude of many throughout the world today, both inside and outside the ranks of organized religion, whether they ever heard of Confucius or not.

There is a growing belief that it is not good for people to be preoccupied with what takes place after death; that, after all, the worthwhileness of life is not a matter of duration but of content, not a matter of extent but of depth and intensity.

The six historic answers to our query can be expressed thus:

Yes, we live on in the bodies of our children.

We live on if our own bodies after death remain intact.

We live on because of the resurrection of our bodies on the Day of Judgment.

We live on only if we eat the body of divinity.

We live on because the body is but one of several abodes of the soul which is eternal.

We should take better care of our bodies and souls whether we live on after death or not.

It seems to me that organized religion has greatly exaggerated the importance of the hope immortal as a motivation for ethical behavior. There have been many tyrants and scoundrels who have held it and many prophets and humanitarians who have not — all the way from Lucretius, the

Roman poet, to Clarence Darrow, the American champion of justice and liberty for the oppressed.

The Jewish people, for example, had no faith in a life beyond the grave until after their contact with Zoroaster's philosophy during the period of the Exile, and after their contact with Greek thought during the Grecian occupation of Palestine. But even since that time down to the present, the Jewish people have never laid much stress on this aspect of their faith. They surely have not been preoccupied with it. But who would venture to contend that they have been lacking in ethical inspiration, or deficient in the zest of living, or indifferent to the claims of truth and righteousness? They have lived as intensely and creatively as any group of people in all human history.

My own point of view on the question is pretty much that of the majority of religious liberals today. I believe a combination of the historic answers given by ancient Israel, ancient India, and Confucius. I agree with ancient Israel that the hope of living on through one's children and the work of one's hands is a very real and inspiring thought. Is there anything more? I agree with Confucius that we know so little about our life here that it is idle to dwell overmuch on what is to happen after death, and that it behooves us, therefore, to make the most of life while we have it.

An immortality dependent upon preserving the form and likeness of the human body, or upon partaking of the sacramental flesh and blood of deity, does not make sense to my mind, and is utterly devoid of ethical significance.

The coming of a day of general resurrection strikes me as most unlikely. That is, of course, an understatement. Either our life goes on after death, or it does not go on at all. But in either event, there is nothing to fear. There will be no agony of disappointment because if life does not continue we shall not be aware of disappointment. I am strongly in-

clined to believe, however, that it does go on. In fact, the
longer I live, the firmer becomes my faith that there is a life
within man that bears the image of eternity and is not involved in the dissolution of the human body. The soul is an
intrinsic part of the creative Power of this universe and
cannot be destroyed. We are the sons of God and jointly
responsible with him for molding the shape of things to come.
Death is not a wall but a door leading to other mansions and
dimensions. Some of our dearest loved ones and closest
friends have passed through that door. Sometime, somewhere, somehow, some of us hope to find some kind of re-
union with them. The poet-preacher, Frederick L. Hosmer,
has summed up my own faith very well in these words of his
inspiring hymn:

> I came not hither of my will
> Or wisdom of mine own:
> That higher Pow'r upholds me still,
> And still must bear me on.
>
> I knew not of this wondrous earth,
> Nor dreamed what blessings lay
> Beyond the gates of human birth
> To glad my future way.
>
> And what beyond this life may be
> As little I divine,—
> What love may wait to welcome me,
> What fellowships be mine.
>
> I know not what beyond may lie,
> But look, in humble faith,
> Into a larger life to die
> And find new birth in death.
>
> Upon his providence I lean,
> As lean in faith I must;
> The lesson of my life hath been
> A heart of grateful trust.

21

Religious Liberalism and the Free Mind Principle

We stand for Religion against the rising tide of secularism in a world that has very largely accepted a materialistic if not an atheistic philosophy.

We stand for Tolerance in a world that is increasingly dominated by sectarianism and bigotry.

We stand for Liberty in a world that has at many points surrendered to arbitrary authority.

We stand for Reason in a world that has succumbed to an alarming degree to blind emotionalism.

We stand for the Ethics of Jesus in a world that seems to have reverted to the ethics of the jungle.

We stand for Individual Responsibility in a world that puts its trust chiefly in mass movements and a regimenting State.

We stand for these things uncompromisingly and openly.

We do not expect to find it an easy position to hold.

But we believe that we shall have many powerful allies when the real issues are made clear.

— FREDERICK MAY ELIOT

SOME MAY WONDER WHY the Liberal Faith is placed in the category of world religion instead of being regarded as merely one of the several expressions of Christianity.

It is because it represents so pronounced a departure from the orthodox doctrines of the main body of Christian

197

Churches as to amount to a new religion, just as in the case of Christian Science. The World Council of Christian Churches which met at Amsterdam not long ago, invited the Christian Scientists to be officially represented, whereas it did not send a similar invitation to the Unitarians or Universalists, or any of the other liberal fellowships, knowing full well that none could subscribe to the creedal basis of the Council which requires belief in Jesus of Nazareth as the God and Savior of mankind. The World Council seems to hold the Christian Science Church less of a threat to the historic Christian dogmas than either the Unitarian Church or the Universalist Church.

Both churches, however, sprang from the loins of Christianity and especially from the loins of Congregational Christianity. Most Unitarians, Universalists and other religious liberals sincerely believe that they preach a gospel nearer to that *of* Jesus than those churches which make so much of the religion *about* him.

The religion *about* Jesus the religious liberals regard as largely a pagan corruption foisted on early Christianity because of the necessity of competing with the superstitious cults which flourished throughout the Roman world in the centuries immediately before and after the beginning of the Christian era.[1]

According to definitions to be found in several dictionaries, both Unitarians and Universalists belong in the category of Christian denominations. And yet the word "Christian" has been so long and so widely associated with certain theological dogmas which they can no longer honestly accept that they do not feel unduly disturbed when others refuse to call them by this name. For, as they interpret the New Testament, even Jesus, were he living and preaching as he once did, would be refused the name of Christian by the Catholic and orthodox Protestant Churches.

For, nowhere in the first three gospels, liberals hold, is

there any evidence that Jesus equated himself with Deity, or even looked upon himself as a perfect man. When someone addressed him as "Good Master," he protested, saying, "Why callest thou me good? None is good save one, even God." Unitarians and Universalists and several religious groups of similar faith, such as the Ethical Culture societies, are not much disturbed when others refuse to call them Christians. In fact many of them, while acknowledging an enormous debt to both Christianity and Judaism, would forge beyond the limitations of either religion and achieve a truly universal faith — preferring to label themselves simply as religious liberals. They would give their allegiance not to any one religion but to the truth behind all religions.

They would have men unite, not on a common creed, but on the basis of "The Free Mind Principle." They would agree, "not to think alike, but all alike to think," to search out the truth in sincerity and humility. They regard uniformity of belief both unattainable and undesirable, and would insist only upon "unity of the spirit amidst diversity of belief."

Their ideal is the genuine free spirit who strives to give his supreme allegiance to the truth as he sees it, and who confesses to no other equal allegiance, however short he may come from actually living up to his ideal in practice. They recognize that such free spirits can be found in nearly every religion. They are anxious to extend the right hand of fellowship to all liberals, whether they call themselves Confucianists, Hindus, Buddhists, Catholics, Protestants, Jews, Parsees, Moslems, Christian Scientists or followers of Baha'u'llah.

They believe that there are numerous people in the world who, while giving nominal support to some hidebound creed or authoritarian tradition, are vitally concerned in searching out the real truth that makes men free. The genuine liberal, if in the Christian tradition, will recall the words of Samuel T. Coleridge, who said: "He, who begins by loving Christianity better than truth, will proceed by loving his own sect or church better than Christianity, and end in loving himself better than all." Substitute Mohammedanism, Hinduism, Christian Science, Buddhism or any other name for Christianity, and, no matter what the object of loyalty, if it be preferred above the truth, disastrous consequences to the mind and soul and society of man are bound to follow: stultification to the mind; enslavement to the soul; and confusion to the society of man.

He who is ready to accept the truth, the whole truth and nothing but the truth, without flinching or hedging, who overcomes all reluctance to face the realities of life and their full consequences, he alone is entitled to the name of a free and independent spirit.

If truth should say there is little evidence as yet for the existence of God, then the free and independent spirit is prepared to be an agnostic. If truth should say there are few grounds for the hope of immortality, he is required by the logic of his position to adjust his hopes to this knowledge. If truth should say that the victory of good over evil is not universally guaranteed by the nature of the universe, he must be ready to conduct himself accordingly. If truth should say there is no meaning to human existence except the meaning that human beings read into it, by their own courage and devotion, the free and independent spirit replies, "Very well, then; I shall make the best possible adjustment to the situation that I can."

Whatever the truth may be, he wants to know it and face it squarely. He has no infantile desire to live in a world of illusion. He would rather be an inquiring Socrates and unhappy than a happy fool living in a fool's paradise. So far as he is concerned, there is no dark corner in life which should be kept dark. There is no tabooed subject which should not be explored. There is no sacred territory which men and angels should fear to tread. There is no golden time when "Ignorance is bliss and 'tis folly to be wise." To know the truth, regardless of the price he has to pay, is his supreme passion and concern. The only real fear he has is the fear of coming face to face with truth and not being able to recognize it; a wholesome dread of passing by on the other side; an ever-present concern lest he betray the very cause he is pledged to serve. This is why the genuine free spirit is ever alert and diligent in his search for truth.

Like the lookout on a transatlantic liner, he would eagerly scan the horizon for every sign or signal of truth in distress. Like the trained detective he would follow every clue and trail until he has tracked an error to its lair. Like the treasure-hunter in the gospel story, he would sell all to purchase the field that contains the pearl of great price. Like the alert attorney before the bar of justice, he would vigorously cross-examine every witness, saint and sinner, poet and scientist, from the humblest and meanest citizen to see what each has to offer as valid testimony. Like one trained in scientific research, he would carefully scrutinize the sources of his information; be on guard against propaganda and pious frauds; read between the lines of his newspapers and magazines for the slanted story; make due allowance for the fact that many sincere people are amazingly gullible and unconsciously become the victims of the printed word and the loudly shouted slogan.

Secondly, because he is an honest seeker after the truth, he would be friendly toward all other honest seekers after the truth. He may discover that the quest leads him in one direction, while it leads his neighbor in the opposite, but he will not therefore refuse his neighbor the courtesy of recognition as they go their separate ways. Surely, he will not descend to persecuting his neighbor, no matter how foolish his folly may seem, lest he make the mistake of stopping the mouth of some new prophet of the truth. He will recall the sad experience of the apostle Paul, who once hounded the cause which he was later destined to champion. Accordingly, no matter how much others may disagree with him in opinion, no matter how far wrong they may seem to be; as long as they are sincere and honest in following the truth as they see it, he will not refuse them the right hand of fellowship, nor make light of their endeavor.

Thirdly, the genuine liberal spirit would be full of understanding and cautious in his judgments. He would certainly bear in mind that truth is not the same yesterday, today and forever, that it changes with time and place and person; that what may have been true for one age may not be true for another; that what may work on one side of the Pyrenees may not work on the other side; that what may be meat for one individual may be poison for his neighbor; that what may be outworn ritual today could have been sincere worship yesterday.

The honest seeker after truth would not overlook the obvious probability that no one person and no one group of persons, no one age or clime or religion has ever had a complete monopoly of the truth; and that those who have made the most arrogant claims in this respect have often been the most empty-handed.

Fourthly, the true liberal will be eager to recognize the marks of a free spirit even in religions other than his own.

When Confucius says, "Ideas are not to be accepted because uttered by the lofty nor rejected because uttered by the lowly," the true liberal agrees.

When the Chinese philosopher Mo Ti says, "The meaning of every conception or belief or policy lies in what kind of conduct or character it is fitted to produce," the true liberal again approves.

When Lao-tse vows, "I will be sincere to those who are sincere, and to those who are not sincere, I' will also be sincere"; when Akhnaton causes his God to say, "I have set truth in my inward parts and falsehood is my loathing, and they

that worship me must worship me in truth"; when Lord
Krishna describes his ideal human being as "one possessed
of charity which spieth out no man's faults and showeth
tenderness toward all that suffer"; when Buddha declares,
"Never does hatred cease by hatred, hatred ceases by love";
when Zoroaster observes, "Know well that a hundred holy
temples of wood and stone have not the value of one understanding heart"; when Jesus declares, "The Kingdom of
Heaven is within you. . . . Love ye one another even as I
have loved you"; when Micah sums up the Hebrew prophets
by asking, "What doth the Lord require of thee, but to do
justly, and to love mercy, and to walk humbly with thy
God?"; when Mohammed lays down the principle that "no
one is a true believer until he loves for his brother what he
loves for himself"; when Baha'u'llah proclaims, "The gift
of God to this enlightened age is the knowledge of the oneness of mankind and the fundamental oneness of religion";
when Gandhi stakes his life on the principle that "the values
we seek in the goal should first appear in the means we
employ"; and when Mary Baker Eddy repeats again and
again the saying of Jesus, "Ye shall know the truth and the
truth shall make you free," but, more especially, when she
gave the example of daring to think for herself even though
it meant abandoning the faith in which she was reared — in
all these instances, the true liberal recognizes the liberal
point of view, even amidst an otherwise authoritarian religion. The true liberal appreciates that no age, no clime,
no religion has been without some witness to an emancipating
faith.

He searches the scriptures of all religions for truth, but
he does not stop there. He searches classical literature, composed outside the domain of all religion. He listens to the
wisdom stored up in the cherished customs and traditions of
mankind. He turns to modern scientific inquiry and historical research, and asks what have these to disclose. But, above

all, he consults his own experience and his own reason; and then goes forth to tell his friends and neighbors what he has found.

For he is eager to publish the truth abroad, and this he would do with courage and yet with kindliness, knowing only too well that there are spiritually sick people in this world who cannot stand the full shock of truth. For them, he modulates his voice, and perhaps even his vocabulary, but not the content of his conviction.

He is likewise eager to live the truth as he sees it, to put its principles into practice in his daily affairs on the assumption that only those who do the will of Truth shall know of the doctrine. And when life comes to a close and the quest for truth is cut short, his is the profound satisfaction of feeling that whatever may happen to the content of his discoveries, there is something of immortal and permanent value even in the quest itself. The path he has followed may later prove to be a blind alley, but if his exploration has been thorough and painstaking, his service will be real and abiding.

The methods employed by Francis of Assisi to dispense charity have been long since out of date, but his compassion will inspire forever. The social program of the late Leo Tolstoy is of doubtful present value, but his moral and intellectual integrity was and is a substantial contribution to mankind. The biology of Professor Louis Agassiz of Harvard University has long since been superseded but his passionate pursuit of the secrets of nature will remain a thrilling chapter in the story of scientific research. The theology of John Henry Newman, one of the shining lights in the Oxford movement of the nineteenth century, is no longer valid for most religious liberals, but the prayer which he wrote in the midst of his spiritual quest will continue to be the prayer of the earnest seeker after truth for generations to come, as it was the prayer of the late Mahatma Gandhi. John Henry Newman was such a wistful seeker after truth that he was able to personify her and give her the attribute of kindliness. He was not an old man, thinking of death, but a young man with most of his life still before him when he wrote the hymn which has been sung around the world:

> Lead, kindly Light, amid th' encircling gloom,
> Lead thou me on.
> The night is dark, and I am far from home,—
> Lead thou me on
> Keep thou my feet; I do not ask to see . . .
> The distant scene, — one step enough for me.

The "kindly Light" led John Henry Newman into the Roman Catholic Church. The same "kindly Light" led the late Roman Catholic Archbishop, Gregor Aglipay, into the Unitarian fellowship. It led the late Clarence Darrow out of the Unitarian fellowship in which he was born into the society of the materialists. It led the late Annie Besant out of the society of the materialists into the faith of Theosophy.

The duty of everyone to follow the truth as he sees it — but not to despise anyone else because he does not see the truth in the same light — this is what religious liberals mean by the "Free Mind Principle," a principle which, they believe, constitutes the most hopeful basis of world peace and understanding: "Unity of the spirit amidst diversity of belief."

A common theology or a common ideology or a common economic system or a common philosophy are not absolutely necessary as foundations of world law and order. But the will "to live and to let live," the will to respect one another's rights in spite of all differences, is the minimum requirement. If to this will to respect one another could be added the will to love one another also, mankind could then go on to build a civilization beyond even the fondest dreams of the seers and prophets of all the ages. Sooner or later, this *must* and *will* be done.

22

The Religious Foundation for the New World Order

> But the thing a man does practically believe . . .
> concerning his vital relations to this mysterious uni-
> verse . . . is in all cases the primary thing for him,
> and creatively determines all the rest . . . if you tell
> me what it is, you tell me to a very great extent what
> the man is, what the kind of things he will do is.
> Of a man or of a nation we inquire, therefore, first
> of all, what religion they had.
>
> — THOMAS CARLYLE

NOW THAT THE MOST DEVASTATING WAR in human history is
behind us, we must make secure the foundation of the new
world order that is to be.

The foundation of any world order, whether old or new,
is man's attitude towards the universe in which he lives and
moves and has his being. Tell me what it is that the majority
of men really believe about the nature of the universe, and I
will tell you what kind of social order they are likely to set up.
When the ancients asked what it was that upheld the world,
they were told that the world rested on the shoulders of a
giant named Atlas. When they further inquired what it was
that Atlas stood upon, they were informed that the giant's
feet were planted on the back of a huge turtle. My contention is that theology, or man's belief about the nature of the
universe, is the turtle of Atlas — the real foundation upon
which man's world eventually rests.

Every person has a theology, whether he knows it or not, whether he can describe it or not, and this is the most important thing about him. It is his dominating philosophy of life which constantly guides and controls his daily conduct. It is the motivating center of all his acting and thinking. It usually functions on a subconscious plane, but it is sometimes possible for an individual to phrase it in clear and unmistakable language. A man, or the social order he builds, can be no better than his theology, although both can fall short of its full implication. The reality behind the universe is probably the same — yesterday, today and forever — but man's basic conception of what this reality is has undergone several revolutionary changes which have been reflected in corresponding changes in the social order. Thus theology and the political institutions of mankind have pretty much walked together throughout the ages — not arm in arm, to be sure, for the political institutions have generally lagged behind theology and have had a tendency to keep it from making greater progress. The two, however, are vitally related, very much as cause and effect, though partly as effect and cause.

There was a time, for instance, when man's basic attitude towards the universe was one of fear and apprehension. The reality behind our life was thought to be a devil who must be avoided or placated. The unseen world was peopled with a host of arbitrary spirits, mostly evil and predatory. Hobgoblins, fiends and demons blocked the path of man whichever way he turned. They were always ready to spoil his plans, defeat his efforts, blast his hopes or take his life.

Man's dominating motive at that time was to escape the wrath of a malicious, supernatural order — to hide from it in sackcloth and ashes, if necessary, to buy it off with bribes and sacrifices, to deceive it with trickery and falsehood. Naturally there was little place in primitive man's religion for love and happy adoration. The universe was deemed hostile and man its convenient and legitimate prey. What wonder, then, that the social ethics of that time was brutal and cruel and revengeful. What wonder that every man's hand was against his neighbor, for every man had to look out for himself while the devil took the hindmost. What wonder that organized religion gave its allegiance to witch doctors and exorcists. What wonder that the prevailing system of economics was more or less cannibalistic in character. One had to eat one's fellow man before one's fellow man did the eating. A fearful theology gave rise to a social order that was literally shot through with fear and insecurity.

Gradually man's attitude towards the universe changed. The reality behind it came to be regarded as potentially benevolent, but still more or less arbitrary and therefore still to be feared and, in addition, to be obeyed as subjects fear and obey a king. This reality bore various names, such as Yahweh, Jupiter, Vishnu and Horus.

Man's chief motive in life now becomes the praise and obedience of a supersovereign in the skies. Man has rights and privileges, but they are all handed down from above. When Yahweh tells Abraham to pull up stakes and journey into a far country, there is no choice for him but to go. When he suggests to Elijah that the prophets of Baal should be slain, his wish is law. The reality behind the universe is powerful and partial. He picks out certain people for special favors, and it is the part of wisdom to keep in his good graces, for these special favors may be withdrawn at any moment. Therefore the people must be careful at all times to preserve a respectful attitude towards the source of their blessings. God is an absolute monarch; men and women are his subjects. There is no call here for love, no place for self-respect. Man must bow mighty low or he will suffer direful consequences.

Is it any wonder that with this kind of theology ruthless rulers should rise to power, or that feudalism should become the dominant economic system, or that absolutism should prevail among the priesthood, or that servility should characterize the masses of the people? The idea of an absolute monarch at the head of the universe begets a cringing attitude towards life. It is bound sooner or later to produce obedient but unthinking underlings. The foundation of the medieval Mohammedan empire was a god of arbitrary power.

Such a god was the foundation of Japan's recent extensive domain. This was why the average Japanese was ready to die for his emperor. His emperor was looked upon as the Son of Heaven and could therefore do no wrong. Whatever rights the Japanese people enjoyed, they had from the emperor's hand. Their one supreme duty was to obey orders. Subservience to his will characterized all the institutions of Japan from the custom of hara-kiri practiced by the higher castes to the regular visitation of Shinto shrines on the part of the common people.

Let me now mention another drastic change that has taken place in man's basic theology and show how it has been reflected in the social order. I refer to the concept that God is a Heavenly Father and that the people of this earth are his children. The universe becomes more benevolent and less arbitrary. God is still to be obeyed, but in addition he is to be loved. He knows what is best for us. He has numbered all the hairs of our heads. He watches the sparrow's fall. He provides for all our wants — food, drink, raiment. The Heavenly Father knoweth that we have need of these things, even before we ask. He punishes us for our wrongdoing only as an earthly parent reproves his child, namely, to do us good, and he forgives us when we repent. It is not his will that any of his little ones should perish. Like a shepherd, he maketh us to lie down in green pastures and leadeth us beside the still waters. God as father or shepherd — this has been the fundamental faith of millions in the past. It is still the fundamental faith of millions today.

What wonder that there has been a steady mollification of

the institutions of mankind, especially in Western civilization where this kind of theology has been more widespread than elsewhere. What wonder that governments have become paternalistic, yielding much of their former absolutism, while the stronger nations have assumed mandates and protectorates over weaker peoples. What wonder that papacy and episcopacy should develop as the prevailing ecclesiastical order. What wonder that philanthropy should grow apace and the colored races become the white man's burden. Let paternalism be thought to preside at the center of the universe, and paternalism will permeate the institutions of mankind.

Industry in America and Great Britain has been increasingly surrendering the arbitrary power it once exercised. It is rapidly becoming more benevolent towards those committed to its care. Employees are being given bonuses and clinical service. Employers have been taking a real interest in their departments of social welfare. The idea of trusteeship is capturing the holders of great wealth.

How long has the concept of a benevolent Heavenly Father been in existence? At least three thousand years and probably a good deal longer, but it is only in the last few decades that the economic order has begun to react to the clear implications of the concept. As the seasons lag behind the ascending or receding sun, the social institutions of mankind lag behind theology. A new, commanding idea rises on the horizon of human thought before the old has finished its work.

Another significant change in man's basic attitude towards the universe is now about to take place. Indeed, it is already taking place, and sooner or later it is bound to bring about revolutionary changes in the social order. The reality that men have agreed to call by the general name of God is no longer regarded as an enemy to be feared and placated (except in certain backward areas of the earth), nor is it looked upon as an absolute monarch whose arbitrary wish is law (except among the Japanese, whatever die-hard Nazis may be left, and certain Mohammedan and Hindu sects), nor is the dependent relation of children to a benevolent father an adequate description of the newly developing attitude in the world today. Men and women in many countries are coming more and more to look upon the universe as a friendly partner. Man needs God, to be sure, but God also needs man. God and man are of the same essence. They are co-creators in a cosmic task, co-partners in a universal enterprise, co-sharers in a common destiny. The old attitude of fright is going; the old servile attitude is going; even the filial attitude is on its way out. Fear, subserviency and even dependency are giving way to the spirit of self-respecting co-operation. God does not ask man to work for him or under him, but *with* him. Man does not expect God to work for him either, or over him, but *with* him. Dictatorship at the heart of the universe, whether infernal, imperial or paternal, is gradually being rejected, thanks in large part to the revelations of modern science, thanks also to the democratic implications of Hebrew prophecy. Man is standing up today and looking at the universe more and more without either prostrate deference or reckless defiance. The universe is something that calls for co-operation. God, the life behind it, is a great companion who must be understood and assisted, whose habits of working must be learned in order that man may understand how to work best with him.

Let demonism, absolutism and paternalism depart from the center of man's universe of thought, and demonism, absolutism and paternalism will eventually depart from all his social institutions.

There is, without doubt, a new and revolutionary theology coming into being throughout the world today. It is being given conscious expression by churchmen, scientists and sociologists alike. Postulate partnership at the heart of the universe and the spirit of partnership is bound to permeate the whole of life.

The idea of a co-operative, democratic God is the only foundation for any new world order that is to meet the growing needs of mankind. Already, as a result of today's changing theology, I foresee certain inevitable transformations in the society of tomorrow.

For one thing, I foresee more, not less, democracy in government. Kings and dictators are doomed. Men and women are going to insist more and more upon the duty as well as the right of governing themselves. They are going to reach the conclusion that no one is good and wise enough to do it for them. They are going to insist upon the privilege of making their own political mistakes and will not permit this privilege to be monopolized by a few.

I also foresee more and more democracy in the world of industry and commerce. Men and women are going to insist upon a greater degree of control over their own economic destiny. Slavery will have to go. Exploitation will have to go. Even trusteeship will have to go. Partnership in the management as well as in the emoluments of industry and commerce is coming sooner or later.

I also foresee more democracy in our family life. The benevolent patriarch who once dominated the domestic scene has already lost his position of authority. All parental dictatorship will go out of fashion. Motherhood will become voluntary. Children will be accorded not only more rights but also more responsibilities. Family life will become more and more a co-operative enterprise of equal personalities.

I also foresee more and more democracy in education. The acquisition of knowledge will become a joint undertaking of pupil and teacher. "Wisdom," as Professor Harry A. Overstreet prophesies, "will not be ladled out like soup that has already been prepared by master cooks. Everyone will be encouraged to taste the broth and add his own seasoning, before it is swallowed." The method of forum discussion will supplant the platform lectures. Teachers will appeal to the authority of experimentation and listen to the wisdom of children, as well as impart their own.

There is likewise going to be more and more democracy even among the churches of mankind. The magic medicine man and the witch doctor have all but disappeared. The infallible priest who holds the keys of heaven and hell is still with us, but his days are definitely numbered. The paternal pastor who watches over his people as a shepherd over his flock is also due for a loss of prestige. The religious leader of the new tomorrow will be compelled to be more democratic in his manner and habits. He will not presume to preach a sermon on some controversial subject without giving those who disagree with his conclusions a fair chance to do so. He will be obliged to regard the proclamation of religious truth as a joint endeavor, a mutual undertaking and a common responsibility of layman and minister. The voice of the layman will be heard more frequently in the pulpit, and the unchallenged sermon will give way to the religious round-table conference and the open forum.

Finally, I foresee more and more democracy in the race relations of mankind. The assumption of ethnic superiority is bound sooner or later to be liquidated in favor of mutual respect and cultural co-operation. There will be no chosen people, no white man's burden, no subject races and no second-class citizenship. All peoples are going to be compelled to recognize their interdependence and to acknowledge the special contribution of each to the welfare of the rest.

All these things I foresee as the logical result of a new attitude towards the universe which is gradually taking possession of the minds and imaginations of men today, in America and Great Britain, in China and Russia — yes, even in Germany and Japan. Man's attitude towards the universe has vitally molded the social order in the past. His new attitude, in my judgment, will eventually create a new earth.

Here, in the concept of a co-operating, democratic Deity, is the religious foundation of the New World Order that is to be — an order we both pray and assume will include some working federation of all countries (towards which the United Nations may well lead us), one that is *sufficiently strong* to insure the practical outlawry of war, the effective social control of atomic power for constructive ends and, above all, the lifting of the terrible burden of armament and anxiety that has weighed so heavily upon the life of our times. Sooner or later, a co-operative world is bound to come. It is the only intelligent answer to the growing needs and expanding vision of mankind.

I see a world where thrones have crumbled and where kings are dust. The aristocracy of idleness has perished from the earth.

I see a world without a slave. Man at last is free. Nature's forces have by Science been enslaved. Lightning and light, wind and wave, frost and flame, and all the secret, subtle powers of earth and air are the tireless toilers for the human race.

I see a world at peace, adorned with every form of art, with music's myriad voices thrilled, while lips are rich with words of love and truth: — a world in which no exile sighs, no prisoner mourns: a world on which the gibbet's shadow does not fall: — a world where labor reaps its full reward; where work and worth go hand in hand; where the poor girl trying to win bread with the needle — the needle that has been called "the asp for the breast of the poor," — is not driven to the desperate choice of crime or death, of suicide or shame.

I see a world without the beggar's outstretched palm, the miser's heartless, stony stare, the piteous wail of want, the livid lips of lies, the cruel eyes of scorn.

I see a race without disease of flesh or brain — shapely and fair, the married harmony of form and function — and as I look, life lengthens, joy deepens, love canopies the earth, and over all in the great dome, shines the eternal star of human hope.[1]

Notes

1. THE REASONABLENESS OF CONFUCIUS

Opening Quotation: Miles Menander Dawson (ed.), *The Wisdom of Confucius* (Boston: International Pocket Library, 1932), pp. 13-14.

1. Max Müller (ed.), *The Sacred Books of the East* (Oxford: Clarendon Press, 1885), Vol. XXVII, p. 138.
2. Robert Ernest Hume, *The World's Living Religions* (New York: Charles Scribner's Sons, 1924), pp. 114-115.

2. MO TI AND THE WILL TO PEACE

Opening Quotation: Hu Shih, *The Development of the Logical Method in Ancient China* (Shanghai: The Oriental Book Company, 1922), p. 82.

1. *Ibid.,* p. 78.
2. *Ibid.,* p. 55.
3. Harry Kingman, "Mo Tih — One of the Immortals," *Unity,* Vol. XCIX, No. 20 (August 22, 1927), p. 331.
4. *Ibid.,* p. 332.
5. *Ibid.,* p. 332.
6. *Ibid.,* p. 332.
7. Hu Shih, *op. cit.,* p. 65.
8. Harry Kingman, *op. cit.,* p. 332.
9. Hu Shih, *op. cit.,* pp. 66-67.
10. Harry Kingman, *op. cit.,* p. 332.
11. *Ibid.,* p. 332.
12. *Ibid.,* p. 333.

3. LAO-TSE AND THE INNER LIFE

Opening Quotation: Robert O. Ballou (ed.), *The Bible of the World* (New York: The Viking Press, 1939), Copyright 1939 by Robert O. Ballou, pp. 511-513. The passage quoted has been slightly transposed.

1. *The Sacred Books of the East, op. cit.,* Vol. XXXIX, pp. 34-35.
2. "Lao-tsze," *Encyclopedia Britannica* (11th Edition; Cambridge: at the University Press), Vol. XVI, p. 193.
3. *Ibid.,* pp. 192-193.
4. *Tao Te Ching,* a new translation by Ch'u Ta-Kao. (London: The Buddhist Lodge, 1937), p. 71. By permission.
5. Ruth Cranston, *World Faith* (New York: Harper and Brothers, 1949), pp. 65, 67. By permission.
6. Robert French Leavens and Mary Agnes Leavens (eds.), *Great Companions* (Boston: The Beacon Press, 1941), Vol. II, pp. 322, 323.

7. *Tao Te Ching*, p. 62. By permission.
8. Ruth Cranston, *World Faith*, p. 66. By permission.
9. *Tao Te Ching*, p. 35. By permission.
10. *Ibid.*, p. 46.
11. *Ibid.*, p. 90. Adapted. By permission.
12. *Ibid.*, p. 67. Adapted. By permission.

4. AKHNATON AND THE CONCEPT OF ONE GOD

Opening Quotation: James Henry Breasted, *A History of Egypt* (New York: Charles Scribner's Sons, 1905), pp. 371, 373-4.

1. *Ibid.*, p. 374.
2. Arthur E. P. Weigall, *The Life and Times of Akhnaton* (Edinburgh and London: William Blackwood and Sons, 1911), pp. 283-284.

5. KRISHNA AND THE LAW OF COMPENSATION

Opening Quotation: Robert Ernest Hume (ed.), *Treasure-House of The Living Religions* (New York: Charles Scribner's Sons, 1932), p. 61.

1. James Freeman Clarke, *Ten Great Religions* (Boston and New York: Houghton, Mifflin and Company, 1888), p. 82.
2. On the date of the Bhagavad-Gita, see *The Bhagavad-Gita,* translated and interpreted by Franklin Edgerton, Part 2 (Cambridge: Harvard University Press, 1944), p. 5: "Nor can we date it with any accuracy; all that we can say is that it was probably composed before the beginning of our era, but not more than a few centuries before it. We do know this: it was preceded by a long literary and intellectual activity, covering perhaps a thousand years or even more, and reaching back to the hymns of the Rig Veda itself, the oldest monument of Hindu literature."
3. *Bhagavad-Gita*, Second Adyar Edition, Besant translation. (Wheaton, Ill.: The Theosophical Press, 1947), Seventh and Ninth Discourses. By permission.
4. *Ibid.* Second Discourse. By permission.
5. Ruth Cranston, *World Faith, op. cit.*, pp. 10-11. By permission.
6. Condensed from Robert O. Ballou (ed.), *The Bible of the World*, p. 54.

6. BUDDHA AND THE EIGHTFOLD PATH

Opening Quotation: John Haynes Holmes *et al.*, *Readings from Great Authors* (New York: Dodd, Mead and Company, 1922), pp. 88-89.

1. It is difficult to estimate the number of Buddhist adherents. With reference to China, John B. Noss in *Man's Religion* (New York: The Macmillan Company, 1949), p. 185, note, writes: "Today, although the nominal adherents of Buddhism in China (people who resort to Buddhist shrines or priests at least occasionally) number perhaps 250,000,000 souls, and a Buddhist revival has had some effect in middle China, Chinese Buddhism has lost the force it once possessed; and unless it reacquires pertinence to rapidly changing Chinese needs, it will not long maintain even its present diminishing strength."

7. KING ASOKA AND THE ROCK EDICTS

Opening Quotation: H. G. Wells, *The Outline of History* (New York: The Macmillan Company, 1920), Vol. I, pp. 432-433.

1. Haridas T. Muzumdar, *The United Nations of the World* (New York: Universal Publishing Company, 1942), pp. 166-167. Reprinted by permission of Dr. Haridas T. Muzumdar.

8. ZOROASTER AND THE STRUGGLE AGAINST EVIL

Opening Quotation: L. Griswold Williams (ed.), *Antiphonal Readings for Free Worship* (Boston: The Murray Press, 1933), p. 99.

1. Will Durant, *The Story of Civilization, Our Oriental Heritage* (New York: Simon and Schuster, 1935), p. 369.
2. *Ibid.*, p. 369.
3. Grace H. Turnbull (ed.), *Tongues of Fire* (Baltimore: The Johns Hopkins Press, 1941), Copyright by Grace H. Turnbull, 1941, p. 104.

9. THE HEBREW PROPHETS AND THE HEART OF RELIGION

Opening Quotation: Micah 6:6-8.

1. For various interpretations of the personal life of Hosea see J. M. P. Smith, *The Prophets and their Times*, 2nd Ed., revised by William Irwin (Chicago: The University of Chicago Press, 1941), pp. 70-76; and Robert H. Pfeiffer, *Introduction to the Old Testament* (New York: Harper and Brothers Publishers, 1941), pp. 567-570.

10. SOCRATES AND THE SEARCH FOR TRUTH

Opening Quotation: *The Dialogues of Plato* (Jowett translation), Introduction by Raphael Demos (New York: Oxford University Press, 1920), Vol. I, p. 282. By permission.

1. *Ibid.*, pp. 421, 423.
2. *Ibid.*, p. 501.
3. *Ibid.*, p. 501.

11. JESUS AND THE JOY OF CHRISTIANITY

Opening Quotation: Henry B. Rankin, *Personal Recollections of Abraham Lincoln.* Quoted in *Great Companions*, Compiled by Robert French Leavens and Mary Agnes Leavens (Boston: The Beacon Press, 1939), Vol. I, pp. 100-101.

12. MARCUS AURELIUS AND THE STOIC VIRTUES

Opening Quotation: *The Thoughts of the Emperor M. Aurelius Antoninus*, Translated by George Long. Revised Edition (London: George Bell & Sons, 1885). Book IV, 3, and Book VII, 59, pp. 93, 140.

1. *Ibid.*, Book III, 7 and 4. Adapted, pp. 89, 87.
2. *Ibid.*, Book VI, 47; and Book V, 6, pp. 128, 108.
3. *Ibid.*, Book VII, 9; Book IV, 36; Book II, 1; and Book VI, 42, pp. 132, 101, 78, 126-127.

13. MOHAMMED AND RACIAL EQUALITY

Opening Quotation: M. K. Schermerhorn (ed.), *Sacred Scriptures of World-Religion* (Cambridge, Mass., 1914), pp. 233-234.

1. Grace H. Turnbull (ed.), *Tongues of Fire* (Baltimore: The Johns Hopkins Press, 1941), p. 404.
2. John B. Noss, *Man's Religion* (New York: The Macmillan Company, 1949), p. 708.
3. James Freeman Clarke, *Ten Great Religions* (Boston and New York: Houghton, Mifflin and Company, 1890), p. 453.
4. Ruth Cranston, *World Faith* (New York: Harper and Brothers, 1949), p. 166. By permission.
5. *Ibid.*, p. 155.
6. *Ibid.*, p. 154.
7. *Ibid.*, p. 169.
8. *Ibid.*, pp. 167-168.
9. *Ibid.*, p. 158.

14. FRANCIS OF ASSISI AND THE LADY POVERTY

Opening Quotation: Wade Crawford Barclay (ed.), *Challenge and Power* (New York: Abingdon-Cokesbury, 1936), Copyright by Wade Crawford Barclay, p. 106.

15. BAHA'U'LLAH AND WORLD FEDERATION

Opening Quotation: *The Dawn of the New Day*, Published under the supervision of the American National Spiritual Assembly, p. 14.

16. MARY BAKER EDDY AND THE CONQUEST OF FEAR

Opening Quotation: Mary Baker G. Eddy, *Science and Health with Key to the Scriptures* (Boston: Joseph Armstrong, 1903), p. 288.

1. Lyman P. Powell, *Mary Baker Eddy, a Life Size Portrait* (New York: The Macmillan Company, 1930), p. 40.
2. *Ibid.*, p. 38.
3. *Ibid.*, p. 38.

17. KARL MARX AND THE RELIGION OF COMMUNISM

Opening Quotations: Karl Marx, *The German Ideology*, as quoted in John Bartlett (ed.), *Familiar Quotations* (Boston: Little, Brown and Company, 1937), p. 1071; and Max Beer, *Fifty Years of International Socialism* (New York: The Macmillan Company, 1935), p. 74.

18. GANDHI AND THE POWER OF SOUL FORCE

Opening Quotation: Joseph J. Doke, *M. K. Gandhi: An Indian Patriot In South Africa* (London: The London Indian Chronicle, 1909), p. 84.

1. E. Stanley Jones, "India's Caste System and Ours," *The Christian Century*, Vol. LXIV, No. 34 (August 20, 1947), p. 996.
2. Poem by Karl Ashbridge Cheyney. Used by permission of author.

19. THE GOLDEN RULE IN ALL RELIGIONS

Opening Quotation: from the *Tao Te Ching*, a new translation by Ch'u Ta-Kao (London, The Buddhist Lodge, 1937) , p. 62. Adapted.

1. Various forms of the Golden Rule given in this chapter are found in Alfred W. Martin, *Seven Great Bibles* (New York: Frederick A. Stokes Company, 1930) , p. xvi.
2. Robert O. Ballou (ed.) , *The Bible of the World*, p. 413. Adapted.
3. Edwin Markham, *The Shoes of Happiness and Other Poems* (New York: Doubleday, Doran and Company, Inc., 1934) , p 115. Reprinted by permission of Mr. Virgil Markham.

20. THE HOPE IMMORTAL IN ALL RELIGIONS

Opening Quotation: *The Dialogues of Plato* (Jowett Translation) . Introduction by Raphael Demos (New York: Oxford University Press, 1920) , Vol. I, pp. 422, 423. By permission.

1. Minot J. Savage, *Minister's Handbook* (Boston: George H. Ellis, 1906) , p. 58.
2. Robert O. Ballou (ed.) , *The Bible of the World*, p. 631.
3. John 6:53-58.
4. Conrad H. Moehlman, *Protestantism's Challenge* (New York: Harper and Brothers, 1939) , p. 166.
5. *The Bhagavad-Gita*, translated and interpreted by Franklin Edgerton. Harvard Oriental Series, Vol. 39 (Cambridge: Harvard University Press, 1944) , pp. 100-101.
6. Robert E. Hume (ed.) , *Treasure-House of the Living Religions* (New York: Charles Scribner's Sons, 1932) , p. 73.

21. RELIGIOUS LIBERALISM AND THE FREE MIND PRINCIPLE

Opening Quotation: From the Address of the President at the Annual Meeting of the American Unitarian Association, May 26, 1949, *The Christian Register*, August 1949, p. 36.

1. See Shirley Jackson Case, *The Origins of Christian Supernaturalism* (Chicago: The University of Chicago Press, 1946) .

22. THE RELIGIOUS FOUNDATION FOR THE NEW WORLD ORDER

Opening Quotation: Thomas Carlyle, *Heroes and Hero-Worship* as quoted in *Great Companions*, Compiled by Robert French Leavens and Mary Agnes Leavens (Boston: The Beacon Press, 1939) , Vol. I, p. 109.

1. "Decoration Day Oration, 1882," *The Works of Robert Ingersoll* (New York: C. P. Farrell, 1900) , Vol. IX, pp. 453-454.

Index